Social Issues
in Literature

Suicide in Arthur Miller's
Death of a Salesman

Other Books in the Social Issues in Literature Series:

Social Issues
in Literature

Suicide in Arthur Miller's
Death of a Salesman

Alicia Cafferty Lerner and Adrienne Wilmoth Lerner,
Book Editors

GREENHAVEN PRESS
A part of Gale, Cengage Learning

Detroit • New York • San Francisco • New Haven, Conn • Waterville, Maine • London

Christine Nasso, *Publisher*
Elizabeth Des Chenes, *Managing Editor*

© 2008 Greenhaven Press, a part of Gale, Cengage Learning

Gale and Greenhaven Press are registered trademarks used herein under license.

For more information, contact:
Greenhaven Press
27500 Drake Rd.
Farmington Hills, MI 48331-3535
Or you can visit our Internet site at gale.cengage.com

Articles in Greenhaven Press anthologies are often edited for length to meet page requirements. In addition, original titles of these works are changed to clearly present the main thesis and to explicitly indicate the author's opinion. Every effort is made to ensure that Greenhaven Press accurately reflects the original intent of the authors. Every effort has been made to trace the owners of copyrighted material.

Cover image © Hulton-Deutsch Collection/Corbis.

ISBN: 978-0-7377-4018-9 (hardcover)
ISBN: 978-0-7377-4019-6 (paperback)

Library of Congress Control Number: 2008925181

Printed in the United States of America
1 2 3 4 5 6 7 12 11 10 09 08

Contents

Chapter 3: Contemporary Perspectives on Suicide

Introduction

In Arthur Miller's *Death of a Salesman*, Willy Loman's business motto, "It's not what you do . . . it's who you know and the smile on your face," contradicts the basic tenet of the American Dream, that all Americans have the opportunity to reach their goals through hard work. Furthermore, the importance Willy places on being well liked conflicts with the cold facts and numbers (like travel expenses and product inventory) that his business depends on. His denial of the mechanics behind his dream of being a successful businessman makes his dream unrealized, contradictory, and ultimately distorted.

As soon as the play begins, the stage is set for the theme of the distorted dream. The opening stage directions of the salesman's house illustrate the point: "An air of the dream clings to the place, a dream rising out of reality." This single sentence, while not uttered by any of the characters, hovers above every action and word and is found in what Miller specifies in the stage directions as the house's transparent walls. The hazy, unreal atmosphere represents Willy's destiny and his unfulfilled dream. The description of "a dream rising out of reality" signifies, before a single word has been spoken, that *Death of a Salesman* is a play of contradictions. Miller's technique of exposing the American Dream as a psychological struggle between the two opposing concepts of reality and dreaming lays the groundwork for the contradictory character of Willy Loman.

Miller illustrates the stresses associated with the American Dream, set against a backdrop of late 1940s postwar America. While the postwar period was relatively prosperous, the nation remained haunted by the hardships of the Great Depression and World War II. In his memories, Willy revisits the 1930s, a time of dramatic economic depression that followed the great opulence and materialism of the 1920s. The low confidence level of the nation as a whole, especially in terms of business, reflected on its people—both the consumer, still timid about purchasing, and the salesman, aware of this dilemma, whose confidence was often shot before he walked through the door. The businessman who might have made good on a few handshakes and a wink now has to drive seven hundred miles to sell products, though even such extraordinary efforts might result in the salesman being turned away at every city, like Willy is. Even after the economy has improved, Willy continues to struggle.

This nationwide punctured confidence is personified by Willy. The confusion of going from a period of prosperity through an economic depression and resurfacing back to a steady economy has driven Willy to constantly look toward the future while living in the past, never trusting the present. For Willy there is always the hope of tomorrow, but his refusal to face reality destroys the possibility of a hopeful future. This character flaw shows itself in Willy's interactions with his son Biff. Biff fails in his business interview with Bill Oliver and realizes he cannot live in the business-connections world his father wants for him. He tries to explain this to his father, yet Willy only hears what he wants to. Biff enables his father to maintain his illusions, telling him that he has a lunch meeting with Oliver the next day, a lie his brother, Happy, has encouraged Biff to tell to please their father. Now that Willy, fired from the Wagner Company after thirty-four years, has lost his false pride in his own business, he passes his dreams of success on to Biff. Willy remains blind, even to his death, to the reality that Biff does not want to bear Willy's burden of empty words of success. Willy cannot recognize his son's failures in business, just as he cannot recognize his own.

It is not until after Willy is dead that his wife, Linda, makes the final payment on their house. A house is a concrete achievement and a powerful symbol of the American Dream. As illustrated in the stage directions, the Loman house does not have actual walls, but rather imaginary walls, spaces that act as real walls, as Willy only acts as a salesman. Without fully committing to the role, Willy's dreams of American business success go unrealized. Willy buys into the cartoonlike façade of the salesman—"Be liked and you will never want"—but his friend Charley is the voice of reason in saying to Willy: "The only thing you got in this world is what you can sell."

Chronology

1915

Arthur Miller is born on October 17 in New York City.

1923

Miller attends his first play, a melodrama, at the Schubert Theater.

1928

Miller has his bar mitzvah. His father struggles in his business, and the family moves to Brooklyn, where Miller attends James Madison High School.

1930

Miller becomes a student at Abraham Lincoln High School, where he plays on the football team.

1933

After graduating from Abraham Lincoln High School, Miller attends night school at City College in New York for two weeks.

1933–34

Miller works as a clerk in an auto-parts warehouse. He is the only Jewish employee and experiences anti-Semitism.

1934

Miller begins studying journalism at the University of Michigan, where he reports for and edits the student newspaper, the *Michigan Daily*.

1936

Miller writes the play *No Villain* in six days, for which he receives the Hopwood Award in drama. Following this experience he becomes an English major.

1937

Miller revises *No Villain*, titling it *They Too Arise*. The play earns an award from the Bureau of New Plays and is produced in Ann Arbor and Detroit. His play *Honors at Dawn* wins the Hopwood Award in drama.

1938

Miller's play *The Great Disobedience* receives second place in the Hopwood contest. He again reworks *They Too Arise*, this time naming it *The Grass Still Grows*. Miller graduates with a BA in English. He works with the Federal Theater Project in New York City.

1939

Miller writes the plays *Listen My Children* and *You're Next*. His radio play *William Ireland's Confession* airs.

1940

Miller works with the Library of Congress. He marries Mary Grace Slattery. He writes *The Golden Years*, and his radio play *The Pussycat and the Plumber Who Was a Man* first airs.

1941

Miller works nights at the Brooklyn Naval Yard. He writes two radio plays, *Joel Chandler Harris* and *Captain Paul*.

1942

Miller writes the radio plays *The Battle of the Ovens, Thunder from the Mountains, I Was Married in Bataan, Toward a Farther Star, The Eagle's Nest*, and *The Four Freedoms*.

1943

Miller writes the play *The Half-Bridge*, and the one-act play *That They May Win*, produced in New York City. He also writes the radio play *Listen for the Sound of Wings*.

1944

Miller's daughter, Jane, is born. He writes the radio plays *Bernadine, I Love You, Grandpa and the Statue,* and *The Philippines Never Surrendered.* He publishes *Situation Normal,* a book about his experience touring army camps. Premiering on Broadway, his play *The Man Who Had All the Luck* runs for only four performances but receives the Theater Guild National Award.

1945

Miller's novel *Focus* is published. He writes the article "Should Ezra Pound Be Shot?"

1947

All My Sons premieres and receives the New York Drama Critics' Circle Award and the Donaldson Award. Miller writes the radio play *The Story of Gus.* His son, Robert, is born. He buys a vacation home in Roxbury, Connecticut.

1948

Miller builds the shack in which he writes *Death of a Salesman.*

1949

Death of a Salesman premieres to rave reviews. The play is awarded the Pulitzer Prize, the New York Drama Critics' Circle Award, the Antoinette Perry Award, the Donaldson Award, and the Theater Club Award, among others. His essay "Tragedy and the Common Man" is published in the *New York Times.*

1951

Miller meets Marilyn Monroe. Joseph Buloff translates *Death of a Salesman* for a Yiddish production. The first film production of *Death of a Salesman* is made for Columbia Pictures.

1953

The Crucible premieres and is awarded the Antoinette Perry Award and the Donaldson Award.

1954

The first radio production of *Death of a Salesman* airs on NBC.

1955

The one-act play *A View from the Bridge* premieres in a joint bill with *A Memory of Two Mondays*.

1956

Miller divorces Mary Slattery and marries Marilyn Monroe. He revises *A View from the Bridge* into two acts to be produced in London, England.

1957

Arthur Miller's Collected Plays is published. He is convicted of contempt of Congress for refusing to identify Communists he knows to the House Un-American Activities Committee. His short story "The Misfits" is published in *Esquire*. The first television production of *Death of a Salesman* airs in England.

1958

The U.S. Court of Appeals overturns Miller's contempt conviction. He is elected to the National Institute of Arts and Letters.

1959

Miller receives the Gold Medal for Drama from the National Institute of Arts and Letters.

1961

Miller divorces Marilyn Monroe. The film version of *The Misfits* premieres. Miller records *The Crucible: An Opera in Four Acts* by Robert Ward and Bernard Stambler. A movie version of *A View from the Bridge* is released. Miller's mother, Augusta, dies.

1962

Miller marries Inge Morath. Marilyn Monroe dies, and Miller does not attend the funeral. Miller's son Daniel is born.

1963

Miller's daughter Rebecca is born. His children's book *Jane's Blanket* is published.

1965

Miller is elected president of the literary organization International P.E.N. Ulu Grosbard's Off-Broadway production of *A View from the Bridge* is staged.

1966

Miller's father, Isidore, dies.

1967

Miller's short story collection, *I Don't Need You Anymore*, is published.

1968

The play *The Price* premieres.

1970

Miller's literature is banned in the Soviet Union because of his work to free dissident writers.

1977

Miller petitions the Czech government to halt arrests of dissident writers.

1982

Miller's one-act plays *Elegy for a Lady* and *Some Kind of Love Story* are produced under the title *2 by A.M.* in Connecticut.

1983

Miller directs *Death of a Salesman* at the People's Art Theater in Beijing, China.

1984

Salesman in Beijing, chronicling Miller's time in China, is published. Miller receives Kennedy Center Honors for his lifetime achievement.

1985

Twenty-five million people watch *Death of a Salesman*, starring Dustin Hoffman as Willy Loman, on CBS.

1987

The one-act plays *I Can't Remember Anything* and *Clara* are produced under the title *Danger: Memory!* Miller publishes his autobiography, *Timebends: A Life*.

1990

Everybody Wins, a film based on *Some Kind of Love Story*, is released. The television production of *An Enemy of the People* airs on PBS.

1991

The one-act play *The Last Yankee* is produced. *The Ride Down Mt. Morgan* premieres in London, England. Miller is awarded the Mellon Bank Award for lifetime achievement in the humanities.

1992

Miller's novel *Homely Girl* is published.

1993

The expanded version of *The Last Yankee* premieres.

1994

Broken Glass premieres.

1995

Miller is awarded the William Inge Festival Award for distinguished achievement in American theater. Celebrations of the playwright on his eightieth birthday occur in America and England.

1996

Miller receives the Edward Albee Last Frontier Playwright Award.

1997

A film version of the *The Crucible* starring Daniel Day-Lewis and Winona Ryder opens.

1998

Mr. Peter's Connections premieres. A major revival of *A View from the Bridge* wins two Tony Awards. Miller is acknowledged as the Distinguished Inaugural Senior Fellow of the American Academy in Berlin, Germany.

1999

Death of a Salesman is revived on Broadway for the play's 50th anniversary and wins a Tony Award for Best Revival of a Play.

2001

Miller's one-act play *Untitled* appears in New York. The film version of his novel *Focus* is released. Miller receives a National Endowment for the Humanities Fellowship and the John H. Finley Award for Exemplary Service to New York City.

2002

Inge Morath dies. The play *Resurrection Blues* premieres. Miller receives the International Spanish Award, Premio Príncipe de Asturias de las Letras.

2003
Miller is awarded the Jerusalem Prize. Miller's brother, Kermit, dies on October 17th.

2004
Miller's play *Finishing the Picture* premieres.

2005
On February 10, Miller dies of heart failure in his Connecticut home.

CHAPTER 1

Background on Arthur Miller

The Life and Career of Arthur Miller

Stephen A. Marino

Stephen A. Marino is a professor of English at St. Francis College in Brooklyn Heights, New York. Marino has written extensively on Arthur Miller; he is the editor of "The Salesman Has a Birthday": Essays Celebrating the Fiftieth Anniversary of Arthur Miller's Death of a Salesman and the author of A Language Study of Arthur Miller's Plays: The Poetic in the Colloquial. He is also the founding editor of the Arthur Miller Journal, published by St. Francis College.

In the following selection, Marino details Arthur Miller's childhood and youth, as well as his education and early jobs. Marino writes of the beginning of Miller's playwriting career as well as the publication of his first novel. Acknowledging that Death of a Salesman *is considered "one of the greatest American plays of the twentieth century," Marino describes the ideas, themes, and overwhelmingly positive critical reception of Miller's landmark play.*

Arthur Miller is one of the major dramatists of the twentieth century. He has earned this reputation during a more than sixty-year career in which he wrote his first plays as an undergraduate at the University of Michigan in the 1930s; achieved critical success with dramas such as *All My Sons* (1947), *Death of a Salesman* (1949), *The Crucible* (1953), and *A View from the Bridge* (1955) in the 1940s and 1950s; served as president of the International Association of Poets, Playwrights, Editors, Essayists and Novelists (PEN) and as a delegate to two Democratic conventions in the 1960s and 1970s;

Stephen A. Marino, "Arthur Miller," *Dictionary of Literary Biography*, vol. 266: *Twentieth-Century American Dramatists*, Belmont, CA: Gale Group, 2003. Reproduced by permission of Gale, a part of Cengage Learning.

produced a critically acclaimed autobiography, *Timebends: A Life*, in 1987; and premiered new plays on Broadway and in London in the 1990s. In the twenty-first century Miller remains as active as at the beginning of his career, having published a collection of essays, *Echoes Down the Corridor* (2000), and completed a new play, *Resurrection Blues* (2002). [Miller died in February 2005.] Recipient of the New York Drama Critics Circle Award for *All My Sons, Death of a Salesman*, and *A View from the Bridge*, the Pulitzer Prize for *Death of a Salesman*, Tony Awards for *Death of a Salesman, The Crucible*, and Lifetime Achievement (1999), and the Olivier Award for *Broken Glass* (1994), Miller clearly ranks with the other truly great figures of American drama such as Eugene O'Neill, Tennessee Williams, and Edward Albee.

Miller's Childhood and Its Influences

Arthur Asher Miller was born on 17 October 1915 in Manhattan, the second son of Isadore and Augusta Barnett Miller. His older brother, Kermit, was a businessman, and his younger sister is the actress Joan Copeland. The Millers—his father a Jewish immigrant from Poland, his mother born on the lower East Side of Manhattan to Polish Jewish émigrés—were wealthy from their coat and suit factory, a family business that his father had built up. The Millers lived in upper-middle-class splendor on East 112th Street in a large apartment that Miller describes in *Timebends* as "at the edge of Harlem, six stories above the glorious park, from whose windows we could see downtown, even down to the harbor it seemed." The family owned a chauffeur-driven, seven-passenger "National" automobile and a summer bungalow on the beach in Far Rockaway [in Queens]. However, Isadore Miller's business collapsed, even before the stock-market crash of 1929; the family relocated to Brooklyn in 1928, when Arthur was thirteen. The move was clearly a step down, and the family settled in the Midwood section of the borough in a little six-room house on East Third Street, where Arthur shared a bedroom with his maternal grandfather.

The move to Brooklyn and the onset of the Depression were the most defining events of Miller's youth. Many critics have discussed the autobiographical elements of Miller's work, and his experiences as a teenager and young man in Brooklyn during the Depression are evident in many of his plays. The Brooklyn of Miller's youth, despite the size and population of the borough, was still relatively rural and undeveloped, and Miller's recollections emphasize the pastoral aspect. In *Timebends* Miller recounts the life of his "two pioneer uncles," Manny Newman and Lee Balsam, both salesmen whom Miller later used as prototypes for Willy Loman. They had moved their families to Brooklyn after World War I, almost ten years earlier than his own family. Miller describes the Midwood area as "so empty they could watch their kids walking all the dozen blocks to the school across the scrubby flatlands." Miller often describes the physical transformation of Brooklyn in the era between the world wars, when he witnessed a quick and dramatic change to the wholly urban environment of today.

An Emerging Playwright

Miller attended James Madison and Abraham Lincoln High Schools in Brooklyn, where he was an average student and played on the second squad of the Lincoln football team. In 1932 Miller graduated from Lincoln. His poor grades and his family's finances kept him out of college. For two years Miller worked in a succession of odd jobs as a delivery man for his father, as an on-air tenor for a Brooklyn radio station, and as a stock clerk in the warehouse of an auto-parts supplier, an experience he turned into his 1955 one-act play *A Memory of Two Mondays*. During this time Miller first encountered anti-Semitism, which became a major theme of his later work. After saving the $500 minimum bankbook balance to assure the school he would not become an indigent ward of the state, Miller finally entered the University of Michigan at Ann Arbor in 1934.

Miller worked his way through the university with jobs washing dishes three times a day and feeding three floors of mice in a genetics laboratory. But he maintained a full academic schedule and immersed himself in university life, which then had the reputation of being a hotbed of 1930s leftist political radicalism. He wrote for the student newspaper and majored in English. However, Miller's years at Michigan are most notable as the start of his playwriting career. Miller had known little about the theater, but during these formative years he became aware of German expressionism, [Swedish playwright] August Strindberg, and [Norwegian playwright] Henrik Ibsen, who was a major influence on him. Miller read one-act protest plays about miners and stevedores and was markedly affected by the social protest work of *Clifford Odets*. As a result, Miller twice won the annual $250 Avery Hopwood Award (which Miller called the college's Nobel Prize) for *Honors at Dawn* in 1936 and *No Villain* in 1937; a third play, *The Great Disobedience*, placed second in 1938, the year he finished his A.B. [bachelor of arts degree]

After graduation Miller joined the Federal Theater Project, which employed promising young playwrights at a living wage of $23 per week. He expected to have *The Golden Years*, a drama about Montezuma II and Hernán Cortés, produced, but Congress curtailed the program. This play, which was not produced until a 1987 British radio and television version, was written in response to the growing power of Adolf Hitler and was an early demonstration of Miller's lifelong interest in the social relevance of drama.

At this time, because a high-school football injury had made him ineligible for the draft, he also wrote half-hour radio plays for DuPont's Cavalcade of America, the Columbia Workshop, and U.S. Steel. These radio plays exhibit themes that are evident in later Miller masterpieces. For example, in the radio playlet *The Pussycat and the Expert Plumber Who Was a Man* (1941) one character states: "The one thing a man fears next to death is the loss of his good name. Man is evil in his own eyes, my friends, worthless, and the only way he can find respect for himself is by getting other people to say he's a nice fellow." This proclamation foreshadows similar cries by such Miller characters as Willy Loman, John Proctor, and Eddie Carbone, who value the worth of their names in the eyes of the world.

Miller Starts a Family

To assist the war effort and earn some money, Miller worked in the Brooklyn Navy Yard for two years while continuing to work on his plays. In 1940 he married Mary Grace Slattery, a fellow student and a Catholic, whom he had met at the University of Michigan. They settled in Brooklyn Heights and had two children, Robert and Jane. In early 1943, Miller left the Navy Yard to conduct background research for the screenplay of *The Story of G.I. Joe* (1945), adapted from columns by American war reporter Ernie Pyle. Miller used his research for a book of reportage called *Situation Normal* (1944), his first published book, in which he tried to see a higher purpose operating among soldiers about the aims of World War II.

Miller Writes His First Broadway Play

Miller then turned to his first play produced on Broadway, *The Man Who Had All the Luck* (1944). In 1940 he had written a 360-page novel about a man for whom everything turns out perfectly and who therefore comes to believe he has no control over his own destiny. Failing to find a publisher for the novel, Miller rewrote it as a play, publishing it in *Cross-Section* (1944), a volume of new American writing that included works by other then-unknowns such as Norman Mailer and Ralph Ellison. The play opened at the Forrest Theatre on

23 November 1944 to almost universally negative reviews, and the critics punned unmercifully on the title. It closed after four performances.

Miller has called *The Man Who Had All the Luck* "an argument with God." He says that the crux of the play is: "How much of our fate do we make and how much is accident?" The so-called fantasy relates the story of David Beeves (Frieber in the published version), a young, self-taught garage mechanic, who is successful at everything he attempts and benefits from an unbroken series of fortunate events: his garage becomes a success when the state builds a highway next to it; he is rescued from an inability to repair a valuable automobile by the sudden appearance of an expert mechanic; the father of the girl he loves refuses to allow the marriage but is killed in a timely automobile accident; even David's apparent sterility is overcome when his injured wife gives birth to a healthy son. But instead of reveling in his streak of good luck, David becomes haunted by it, coming to believe that his good fortune must be paid for.

David's good luck is contrasted with the story of his brother, Amos, in whom David's father has invested all his hopes and dreams of turning him into a star baseball player. Their father has taught Amos how to pitch in the cellar of their house, and the result is a technically perfect pitcher who is unable to cope in a real game with men on base. David cannot fathom why his brother, despite his efforts, has failed while David has succeeded. David is further challenged by Shory, a wheelchair-bound character who harangues him with his insistence on man's inability to control his fate.

David challenges his fate by staking his wealth on a mink-breeding ranch. The results seem calamitous when a sudden, violent hailstorm and poisoned feed threaten the animals. His wife insists that David should allow the animals to die, for only then will he be free of his fear and accept responsibility for his own actions. The mink survive because David picks the silkworms (fatal if ingested) off the fish he is feeding them, and he, perhaps, realizes he has some measure of control in his life.

Although a critical failure, *The Man Who Had All the Luck* clearly included strains of plot and themes that Miller used in his later successful plays. The rivalry of two brothers is a major component of *All My Sons, Death of a Salesman, The Price* (1968), and even *The Creation of the World and Other Business* (1972), in which Cain and Abel struggle in the first fraternal battle. Similarly, David's acceptance of responsibility for his actions is a key for other major characters. In his introduction to volume one of his *Collected Plays* (1957) Miller acknowledged the critical failure of *The Man Who Had All the Luck* but realized its importance as a seminal text:

> The play was impossible to fix because the overt story was only tangential to the secret drama the author was unconsciously trying to write. But in writing of the father-son relationship and the son's search for his relatedness there was a fullness of feeling I had never known before; a crescendo was struck with a force I could almost touch. The crux of *All My Sons*, which would not be written until nearly three years later, was formed; and the roots of *Death of a Salesman* were sprouted.

In recent years, critics and theater companies have recognized the importance of Miller's first Broadway play. In 1988 a successful staged reading of *The Man Who Had All the Luck* was given in New York, which led to the publication of a new version in 1989.

Miller Writes a Successful Novel

Disappointed by the reception of *The Man Who Had All the Luck* and convinced he would never write another play, in 1945 Miller wrote and published a novel, *Focus*, one of the first important American works about anti-Semitism. The novel was successful, selling ninety thousand copies. The title

Arthur Miller. The Library of Congress.

possesses literal and figurative meanings for the main character, Lawrence Newman. The Gentile Newman, the personnel
manager of a large company that refuses to hire Jews, is forced
to wear glasses because of failing eyesight. Although the glasses
help him see clearly, his co-workers suddenly view him differ-

ently. The glasses make him look like a Jew, and he becomes the object of discrimination and persecution. His colleagues suspect his real name is Neuman, and he is removed to a back desk. He quits and cannot find another job because of his appearance. Moreover, he becomes an outcast to his neighbors, and his wife, a worker for an anti-Semitic organization, is also accused of being a Jew. His neighbors plan an assault against a Jewish grocer who serves their community. But Newman, emboldened by identification with a man he now sees as a fellow Jew, defends the grocer Finkelstein with a baseball bat against the attack. *Focus* tackles a subject that Miller made a major part of his dramatic canon: all humanity shares a responsibility for the suffering of the Jews. The novel was adapted into a motion picture in 2001, starring William H. Macy and Laura Dern.

All My Sons Is Miller's First Broadway Success

Despite the success Miller had with the novel form, he was determined to write another play and decided if it were not a hit, he would give up playwriting altogether. The result of Miller's self-ultimatum was *All My Sons*, his first Broadway hit and critically acclaimed drama. Miller formed the idea for the play from a story his Midwestern mother-in-law told him about a family in her neighborhood that had been destroyed when the daughter discovered her father had been selling faulty machine parts to the army and reported him to the authorities. Miller decided to transform the daughter into a son, and a play was born.

The drama focuses on Joe Keller, a small factory owner, finally forced to confront his legal and moral crime of knowingly selling defective airplane parts during World War II, which resulted in the deaths of twenty-one pilots. Joe has denied his part in the crime by blaming his business partner, who has been in jail for three years, while Joe has reestablished his successful business. When his cover-up unravels, he can no longer deny the truth, and when he ultimately realizes the ramifications of his crime for his family and society, he kills himself.

Keller's two sons and wife also struggle with the repercussions of his crime. Three years earlier, the pilot son, Larry, deliberately crashed his plane out of shame and guilt after discovering his father's culpability. The other son, Chris, survived the war and witnessed the sacrifices men make for each other. Chris suppresses his suspicions of Joe's crime, works in his plant, and plans to marry Ann Deever, Larry's fiancée and daughter of Joe's jailed business partner. But Chris is shattered when the truth is revealed, and he confronts his own and his father's accountability for denying the crime. The mother, Kate, consciously denies her husband's crime and son's death; although she has known the truth from the beginning, she uses astrology and religion to create the illusion that Joe is innocent and Larry is merely missing in action and coming back.

Miller writes in his *Collected Plays* introduction that *All My Sons* is "designed to bring a man into the direct path of the consequences he has wrought." Miller judges that Joe is a threat to society because "his cast of mind cannot admit that he, personally, has any viable connection with his world, his universe, his society." *All My Sons* established Miller as a realistic social playwright in the Ibsenesque tradition, a reputation that has stuck with him throughout his career. Clearly, *All My Sons* is a "well-made" play with a long exposition, careful attention to plot detail, the device of a concealed letter, hidden truths, and secrets. Many critics have seen parallels to Ibsen's *The Wild Duck* (1884) with its emphasis on the revelation of past action.

With the production of *All My Sons* Miller began his professional and personal association with the motion-picture and stage director Elia Kazan. *All My Sons* ran for 328 performances and received the New York Drama Critics Circle Award. Universal Pictures purchased the movie rights, turning it into a movie with Edward G. Robinson and Burt Lancaster in 1948. Miller was beginning to reap the benefits of his success financially and artistically: he bought a house in Brooklyn Heights, and royalty income gave him a new freedom to create. After researching life in the Italian criminal underworld on the docks, waterfronts, and piers of Red Hook, Brooklyn, which he later used as the raw material for *A View from the Bridge*, Miller turned to writing his masterpiece, *Death of a Salesman*.

Death of a Salesman Is Born

Death of a Salesman had been gestating in Miller for some time. When Miller was seventeen he wrote a story (rediscovered by his mother during the original production of the play) called "In Memoriam," based on his experiences with a Jewish salesman when he was working for his father a few months after graduating high school. Miller also had written a play about a salesman and his family during his time at the University of Michigan. Miller was particularly influenced by the memory of his uncle Manny Newman. In *Timebends* Miller relates how Manny, who later committed suicide, raised his two sons to be competitive alter egos with Miller. Thus, the prototypes of Willy, Biff, and Hap were born.

Miller wanted this play to differ from the tight composition of *All My Sons*. By the spring of 1948 he felt that he could find the form of the play but that he would have to write it in one sitting. He retreated to his country house on four hundred acres in Connecticut, which he had bought the year before, and built a workshop where he could block out the world while he wrote the play. As he labored physically, he contemplated everything he had in his head about the play: the name of the salesman's family, Loman; a death; and the first two lines: "Willy" and "It's alright. I came back." When the tiny ten-by-twelve-foot cabin was completed, Miller sat down one April morning and began. He wrote all day until dark, had dinner, and then went back to his desk until the middle of the night. He had finished act 1. When he lay down to sleep, he realized he had been weeping; his eyes and throat hurt from talking out the lines, shouting, and laughing. It took him six more weeks to complete act 2.

Miller sent the completed play to Kazan, who immediately recognized its merit and together with Miller began the casting of what is now widely considered to be one of the greatest American plays of the twentieth century. Lee J. Cobb played the original Willy Loman, while Mildred Dunnock portrayed his wife, Linda. Kazan also enlisted the services of designer Jo Mielziner, who had created the set for [Tennessee] Williams's *A Streetcar Named Desire* (1947). Miller, Kazan, and Mielziner collaborated to produce innovative staging and a revolutionary set that became legendary in the American theater.

The Play, Its Form, and the Artist's Ideas

Death of a Salesman depicts the last twenty-four hours in the life of Willy Loman, a sixty-three-year-old traveling salesman, who for thirty-six years has plied his trade all over New England. Willy has come to realize that he is a failure and is contemplating suicide. At the same time, he is haunted by an unresolved conflict with his son, Biff, over the latter's discovery of Willy's adultery with a woman in a Boston hotel room. Biff, at thirty-four years old, is a fallen football hero who has flunked out of school, stolen himself out of every job he has had, and led an unsettled existence. As the play opens, he has been ranching out West but has come home to Brooklyn on one of his infrequent visits. A younger son, Hap, is mired in a dead-end merchandise job in a New York department store and wallows in whores and booze. Linda is the seemingly long-suffering, supportive wife and mother but also conveys a strength that neither her husband nor sons possess.

In *Death of a Salesman* Miller created a form that was deliberately opposite to a straight realistic play such as *All My Sons*, in which one event creates the necessity for the next. As Miller explains in his *Collected Plays* introduction, he conceived *Death of a Salesman* with the "concept that nothing in life comes next, but that everything exists together and at the same time within; that there is not a past to be 'brought forward' in a human being, but that he is his past at every moment and the present is merely that which his past is capable of noticing and smelling and reacting to." Working in an expressionistic style that has become known as "subjective realism," Miller simultaneously depicted both the real time of the play and the internal workings of Willy's mind, especially as he recalls events of the past. Miller called these scenes "imaginings," and they are not flashbacks but rather what Miller describes in the *Collected Plays* introduction as "a mobile concurrency of past and present," because linear time is broken down in the play. The overall effect is to convey the dislocation of time in Willy's mind, because as Miller has noted, "In his desperation to justify his life Willy Loman has destroyed the boundaries between then and now."

The original working title for *Death of a Salesman* was "The Inside of His Head." Miller's first idea for the set was of an enormous face, the height of the proscenium arch, which would open so that the audience would see the inside of a man's head, where all the action of the play would occur. Mielziner took this image and designed the now-famous set with a series of three platforms, for the kitchen and two bedrooms, without walls. The Boston hotel room, Howard's office, and the yard scenes were played in the open space downstage. Moreover, Mielziner created surrealistic apartment buildings surrounding and encroaching on the Loman house. Lighting and music helped convey the instantaneous changes in time and place. Furthermore, plaintive, haunting flute music punctuated Willy's musings throughout the play.

Death of a Salesman Opens to Rave Reviews

When the play opened on 10 February 1949 at the Morosco Theatre, the critical reaction was overwhelming. It ran for 742 performances and won a Tony Award, the New York Drama Critics Circle Award, and the Pulitzer Prize. Within a year of its premiere, *Death of a Salesman* was playing in every major city in the United States and within a few years began its incredible run of international productions. Brenda Murphy has concluded that since the first production there has never been a time when *Death of a Salesman* was not being performed somewhere in the world.

Salesman and the American Dream

The enduring universal appeal of *Death of a Salesman* to audiences, theater critics, and scholars lies in its focus on the American Dream as a central theme. For thirty-six years as a traveling salesman Willy Loman has fought to achieve the success that the American Dream promises, and he has accrued the tangible products that signify the dream. However, the intangibles—personal satisfaction, self-worth, and economic security—have eluded him, and the play captures the dramatic moments when Willy confronts this failure. Perhaps this recognition is why most audiences have identified with Willy. When Linda tries to convey to her sons that Willy is "a human being and a terrible thing is happening to him," audiences realize that the same can happen to them.

Willy's failure is based largely on his flawed understanding of what constitutes the American Dream; he confuses his material and spiritual values so that he no longer can differentiate between reality and illusion, as illustrated in his imaginative longings for the idyllic past. He alternately believes that personal appearance, being liked, and contacts are the ways to succeed in the material world. Willy has spent his career with these beliefs but has never been a successful "hot shot" salesman with big commissions. He, therefore, has struggled to make the payments on the tangible items that exemplify the dream: his home, the car, the refrigerator. In addition, Willy possesses spiritual flaws; his adultery and condoning of stealing and cheating signify his moral failings. Willy has transmitted his flawed beliefs to his sons, and as a result both men are failures too. Neither is able to perform the hard work necessary to achieve financial success and personal fulfillment. In contrast, the Lomans' next-door neighbor, Charley, and his son, Bernard, have integrated the material and spiritual; they have succeeded financially through integrity, humility, and studiousness.

Popular and Important Analyses of *Salesman*

Death of a Salesman has been analyzed as a play that critiques the role of capitalism in American society. Certainly, the play illustrates Willy's lifelong dream for economic success while he struggles to compete in the American economic system. At the end of the play, in a "Requiem," Hap expresses Willy's striving for the American Dream in a climactic metaphor that is at the heart of Willy's struggle: "It's the only dream you can have—to come out number one man." Willy's drive to achieve that status illustrates the workings of an American capitalist system based on competition. Although the dream possesses the potent allure of seeming attainable for all, its enchantment masks the competition that in reality does not guarantee its achievement by everyone. Willy himself declares in the first scene that "The competition is maddening," and the play details how he is literally maddened as he fails at his dream to be number one. The very products of the American capitalist system seem arrayed against Willy: his car breaks down, and the refrigerator consumes belts like a "goddamn maniac." But ultimately Willy fails to realize that he actually is competing against himself: that he is responsible for his own failure.

Willy's sons also desire the American Dream. Throughout the play, Hap and Biff detail their relative disappointment in what they have accomplished in life: Biff is torn between his love of the outdoors and his desire for economic success in the city, while Hap is stuck selling in a department store. Both men seek financial success and personal contentment, but they are as confused as Willy about how to achieve these things. By the end of the play, only Biff seems to have become aware of his failings, as he tries to tell Willy to take his "phony dream and burn it." On the other hand, Hap decides to stay in the city in an attempt to show that Willy Loman did not die in vain. As the bearer of Willy's legacy, Hap makes the same mistakes as Willy—especially in perverting spiritual and material values. But Hap does not understand that Willy exalts the acquisition of material possessions without regard for personal conduct, misunderstands the legitimate methods for attaining success, and corrupts his humanity.

Perhaps one of the most intriguing analyses of *Death of a Salesman* has been whether Willy Loman is a tragic hero, and therefore, whether the play is a modern tragedy. Critics have argued on both sides: that Willy's death is merely the pathetic demise of a small man, and conversely, that Willy's death is the consequence of his noble action. A few weeks after the production opened, Miller wrote an op-ed piece for *The New York Times* titled "Tragedy and the Common Man" (27 February 1949) in which he made the case for Willy as a modern tragic hero. Miller maintains that modern literature did not require characters to be royalty or leaders and therefore fall from some great height to their demise, as in the tragedies of other eras. Rather, Miller insists: "I think that the tragic feeling is evoked when we are in the presence of a character who is ready to lay down his life, if need be, to secure one thing—his sense of personal dignity. From Orestes to Hamlet, Medea to Macbeth, the underlying struggle is that of the individual attempting to gain his 'rightful' position in his society." Thus,

Miller argues that a lowly man such as Willy could be considered a tragic hero. (Miller chuckled at those critics who emphasized Loman as a pun for "low man"; he actually took the name from a 1933 movie, *The Testament of Dr. Mabuse.*) "Tragedy and the Common Man" is now widely considered to be an important part of twentieth-century literary criticism. It stands as the first of a large body of dramatic criticism that Miller has produced over a span of fifty years, the most significant output of such writing since George Bernard Shaw.

Death of a Salesman Revivals and Awards

Since the original production there have been many notable revivals of *Death of a Salesman* both in the United States and around the world. A New York revival in 1975 featured George C. Scott as Willy; Dustin Hoffman led a stellar 1984 Broadway production with John Malkovich as Biff; and the Goodman Theater of Chicago mounted a fiftieth-anniversary production that opened on 11 February 1999 at the Eugene O'Neill Theater. That show won Tony Awards for Brian Dennehy as Willy, Elizabeth Franz in a redefining role as Linda, and for Best Play Revival. Miller also won a Tony for Lifetime Achievement. International audiences have never lost their attraction to the quintessentially American struggle of Willy Loman. In 1950 audience members in Vienna wept; Japanese audiences responded with empathy to Willy's fall; and the 1983 Beijing production, which Miller directed, caused tears in the Communist Chinese audiences.

An Overview of *Death of a Salesman*

L.M. Domina

L.M. Domina is an essayist on American dramatic works.

Domina's overview of Death of a Salesman *focuses on the effect that secrets, lies, and feelings of failure have on the Loman family. The issues of infidelity and fear of intimacy are recognized as components of the tangled deceit of the Lomans. Domina concludes that Willy Loman's guilt over secrets he's kept and his sense of failure as a salesman contribute to his suicide.*

Arthur Miller's classic American play, *Death of a Salesman*, exposes the relationship between gender relationships and dysfunctional family behaviors. In this play, the themes of guilt and innocence and of truth and falsehood are considered through the lens of family roles. Willy Loman, the salesman whose death culminates the play, is an anti-hero, indeed the most classic of anti-heroes. According to an article on the play in *Modern World Drama*, Willy is "a rounded and psychologically motivated individual" who "embodies the stupidity, immorality, self-delusion, and failure of middle-class values." While his self-delusion is his primary flaw, this characteristic is not necessarily tragic since Willy neither fights against it nor attempts to turn it toward good. Dennis Welland in his book, *Miller: The Playwright* summarized this view, critiquing critics who believe that "Willy Loman's sense of personal dignity was too precariously based to give him heroic stature." Although he is ordinary and his life in some ways tragic, he also chooses his fate. The article in *Modern World Drama* confirmed that "considerable disputation has centered on the play's qualification as genuine tragedy, as opposed to social drama."

L.M. Domina, "An Overview of *Death of a Salesman*," *Drama for Students*, Belmont, CA: Gale Group, 1997. Reproduced by permission of Gale, a part of Cengage Learning.

Although Willy is dead by the end of the play, that is, not all deaths are truly tragic. The other characters respond to Willy's situation in the ways they do because they have different levels of access to knowledge about Willy and hence about themselves. An analysis of the relationships among these characters' insights and their responses will reveal the nature of their flawed family structure.

Failure Within the Loman Family

According to conventional standards, Biff, the older son of Willy and Linda, is the clearest failure. Despite the fact that he had been viewed as a gifted athlete and a boy with a potentially great future, Biff has been unable as an adult to succeed or even persevere at any professional challenge. Before the play opens, he had been living out west, drifting from one low-paying cowboy job to another, experiencing neither financial nor social stability. Back in New York, he is staying with his parents but seems particularly aimless, although he does gesture toward re-establishing some business contacts. Although one could speculate that the Loman family dynamics in general have influenced Biff toward ineffectuality, as the play progresses readers understand that one specific biographical moment (and his willingness to keep this moment secret) provides the key to his puzzling failure.

Near the end of the play, Bernard, Willy's nephew, asks Willy about this crucial incident. Although Biff had already accepted an athletic scholarship to the University of Virginia, he failed math his last semester in high school; his best option was to make the course up during summer school. Before he makes this decision, Biff visits Willy, who is in Boston on business. According to Bernard, Biff "came back after that month and took his sneakers—remember those sneakers with 'University of Virginia' printed on them? He was so proud of those, wore them every day. And he took them down in the cellar, and burned them up in the furnace. We had a fist fight.

It lasted at least half an hour. Just the two of us, punching each other down in the cellar, and crying right through it. I've often thought of how strange it was that I knew he'd given up his life. What happened in Boston, Willy?" Willy responds defensively: "What are you trying to do, blame it on me?"

A Family Stifled by Lies

What had happened, of course, as Willy subsequently remembers and as he has probably remembered frequently during the intervening years, was that Biff had discovered Willy in the midst of an extramarital affair. In contrast to Linda, who frequently appears with stockings that need mending, this other woman receives gifts of expensive stockings from Willy. The existence of this woman (and perhaps others like her) is one factor contributing to the financial strain of the Loman family. Biff understands this instantly, and he also understands the depth of Willy's betrayal of Linda—and the family as a whole. The trust Biff had given Willy now seems misplaced. Indeed, according to the flashbacks within the play, the young Biff and Happy had nearly idolized Willy, so this betrayal while Biff is yet an adolescent is particularly poignant. As Biff is about to make a momentous life decision, in other words, he is confronted with duplicity from the man he had looked to as a role model. Yet Biff shares this knowledge with no one; instead this secret becomes the controlling element of his own life.

When Biff does attempt to tell the truth, not about Willy's affair but about his own life, Willy and Happy both resist him. "Let's hold on to the facts tonight, Pop," Biff says, indicating that "the facts" are slippery in their hands. The outright lies members of the Loman family tell, that is, come more easily because they also exaggerate some facts and minimize others. Although many of their stories may be eventually founded in truth, that truth is so covered with their euphemistic interpretations that it is barely recognizable. The stories the family has

Miller was married to actress Marilyn Monroe from 1956 to 1961. AP Images.

told have become nearly indistinguishable from the real circumstances of their lives. Trying to separate reality from fantasy, Biff says, "facts about my life came back to me. Who was

it, Pop? Who ever said I was a salesman with Oliver?" But Willy refuses to acknowledge the substance of the question: "Well, you were." Biff contradicts him, as determined to acknowledge the truth as Willy is to deny it: "No, Dad, I was a shipping clerk." Willy still declines to accept this fact without the gloss of embellishment: "you were practically" a salesman.

Later, the conversation among the three men reveals that similar embellishments continue to characterize their lives. "We never told the truth for ten minutes in this house!" Biff proclaims. When Happy protests that they "always told the truth," Biff cites a current family lie: "You big blow, are you the assistant buyer? You're one of the two assistants to the assistant, aren't you?" But Happy continues the family habit: "Well, I'm practically . . ."

Issues with Intimacy

This inability to acknowledge the truth affects the family on many levels but most particularly in terms of their intimacy with one another and their intimate relationships with others. Biff hasn't dated anyone seriously, and Happy is most comfortable with prostitutes. While waiting for Willy at a restaurant, Happy assures Biff that a woman at another table is "on call" and urges her to join them especially if she "can get a friend." Although Happy is clearly a participant in this encounter, he says, "Isn't that a shame now? A beautiful girl like that? That's why I can't get married. There's not a good woman in a thousand." Although Happy and Biff would probably classify their mother as a "good woman," they follow their father's example in seeking out women they won't marry to gratify their egos and then in treating those women as disposable.

Linda eventually responds to her sons with scathing disrespect in part because of the way they respond to other women, but primarily because she assumes they chose to accompany prostitutes rather than to fulfill their dinner plans with their father. "You and your lousy rotten whores!" she says. "Pick up this stuff, I'm not your maid any more," she continues, and then asserts, "You're a pair of animals!" Linda, of course, doesn't realize that Willy, too, whom she accuses her sons of deserting, is guilty of infidelity. Willy's emotional stability is threatened, she believes, in part because of the way his sons respond to him. She fails to consider the possibility that Biff's instability and the immaturity of both Biff and Happy have been affected by Willy's model.

Secrets, Lies, and Feelings of Failure

The most profound secret of the play, however, is of course Willy's apparent obsession with suicide. He has been involved in several inexplicable automobile accidents, and he has perhaps planned to asphyxiate himself by attaching a rubber tube to their gas water heater. Linda has discovered this tube and has revealed her discovery to her sons, but she forbids them from addressing the subject directly with Willy, for she believes such a confrontation will make him feel ashamed. This secret is hence ironically acknowledged by everyone except the one whose secret it is—Willy. When he does finally succeed in killing himself, his act can be interpreted as a culmination of secrets, secrets which are compounded through lies because they have been created through lies. Welland suggested that Willy's suicide results from his affair—"To argue that in these days of relaxed social morals one minor marital infidelity hardly constitutes grounds for suicide is, paradoxically, to add weight to the theme in the context of this play: for Willy Loman it is enough." His affair is certainly one factor in his decision, but it is a factor because he had been found out by his son, and because others are now starting to question him. So although these secrets include his affair(s) and Biff's knowledge of this aspect of his life, they also include his failure as a salesman and the subsequent failures of his sons.

Miller and Others Comment on the Impact of *Death of a Salesman*

Arthur Miller, Robert Falls, and Brian Dennehy, interviewed by Paul Solman

Paul Solman is a business and art correspondent for the long-running public television program NewsHour with Jim Lehrer. *Robert Falls directed and Brian Dennehy starred as Willy in the 1999 Broadway revival of* Death of a Salesman.

From high school productions to Broadway, Death of a Salesman *is one of the most frequently produced plays in the United States. To international audiences,* Death of a Salesman *is among the most familiar American dramatic works. It has been staged numerous times and with great critical acclaim in London and in locations as distant as Beijing, China. In 1999, on the fiftieth anniversary of the play's debut, it was revived on Broadway—again with an all-star cast. In the following excerpt of an interview with Paul Solman, Arthur Miller, Robert Falls, and Brian Dennehy discuss the staying power of* Death of a Salesman *and why its themes still resonate with audiences.*

Paul Solman: February 10, 1949, "Death of a Salesman" starring Lee J. Cobb premiered in New York. Tonight, exactly half a century later, Willy Loman returns to Broadway. . . .

This is the play's third Broadway revival. George C. Scott played Willy in 1975. Dustin Hoffman in 1984. . . .

But off-Broadway, usually way off, "Salesman" has been performed non-stop for five decades. Robert Falls directs the current revival first staged in Chicago's Goodman Theater last fall [in 1998]. . . .

Arthur Miller, Robert Falls, and Brian Dennehy, interviewed by Paul Solman, "An American Classic: Arthur Miller Discusses His Life and Work," *Online News Hour*, February 10, 1999. Reproduced by permission.

Robert Falls: You can go to Kansas City, you could go to Miami Beach, you could go to a college in Utah, you could go to a theater in Japan, you could go to a theater in the Soviet Union, and this play is sitting in the repertoire of the world theaters and of American theaters. It's a play that for 50 years has never lost its popularity.

Inspired by His Uncle

Paul Solman: Playwright Arthur Miller was only 33 when he won a Tony Award and the Pulitzer Prize for "Death of a Salesman" in 1949. The play takes place in Brooklyn during the last 24 hours of Willy Loman's life, as he's [plagued] by his failures and those of his sons, especially the older one, Biff. The idea had come two years earlier when [Miller] bumped into his Uncle Manny, the salesman, after a performance of his first hit play "All My Sons."

Arthur Miller: I was coming out of the theater and there he was—I hadn't seen him in—I don't know—10 or 15 years, and I greeted him and without a word he said the equivalent of "Biff is doing very well."

Paul Solman: Biff, the son of Willy Loman in the play?

Arthur Miller: And I'm using "Biff" but the real name was not Biff. And the idea suddenly struck me that he's living in two different eras at the same time.

Paul Solman: Because he's talking about his son, your cousin?

Arthur Miller: He's talking about his son, my cousin. I haven't seen this man in 15 years, but you see what he was carrying forward was his competitive race between me and his son as of 30 years before.

Paul Solman: And so here you had your play and he's saying to you, "hey, your cousin's doing just as well."

Arthur Miller: Just as well. It was very touching. At the same time, it was miraculous that the human brain could be running on two different tracks like that. So the play is filled with these concurrences where somebody—he's talking to a man that he's playing cards with and at the same time he's talking to somebody who died 25 years before.

Audience Reactions to the Play

Paul Solman: Assailed by voices from the past, exhausted by years of false cheer on the road, Willy is unraveling. He begs his young boss for a desk job at almost any salary, instead he's fired from the only job he's ever had. In the end, Willy kills himself, as Miller's Uncle Manny did, not long after his encounter with his nephew at "All My Sons." For the audience, watching can be almost unbearable.

Brian Dennehy: I see extremely sophisticated, very successful New Yorkers with absolutely no questions at all about who they are, how far they've come, and how right their lives are, I see them dissolve in tears, their shoulders shaking, ready to just go home.

Paul Solman: That's also an apt account of the cast's condition at the end of this three-hour performance. In the preview we saw, Elizabeth Franz, Willy Loman's wife wept so desperately at the end of the play that when the curtain call came, she was still shaking with sobs.

Arthur Miller: Originally, of course, when we first performed and people didn't know what to expect, they didn't applaud at all for a good three, four minutes.

Paul Solman: Three or four minutes?

Arthur Miller: Oh, yeah—and then suddenly would remember to applaud because there were actors behind the curtain. And it would take them several minutes to think about it.

A Cathartic Experience

Paul Solman: For both actors and audience, then, it can be a truly cathartic experience. But why would a 50-year-old play about a pathetic small-time loser still resonate so powerfully?

Robert Falls: You cannot come out of it without going, "I know somebody like that. That's my father, that's my brother, that's my son, that's my uncle." And that's a work of genius to have that happen. . . .

This is about a father who loves his son so much that he sort of passes on all the sort of wrong values, if you're liked, if you're handsome enough, if you're charming enough—it's all about sort of surface appearances. And I think that's still a lesson that we see today. I mean, if anything, we live in a society which is far more disposable than ever, the fact that we're always looking for the newer—the hotter—you're going to be displaced sometime for a younger guy, a younger, more attractive guy than you are. I'm going to be displaced for exactly the same reason.

Questioning the American Dream

Paul Solman: "Death of a Salesman" has lived through its share of historical changes. Written early in the Cold War, its cynical take on the American dream made it a political hot potato. When the film version was made in 1951 starring Frederick March, the studio decided to release it with an accompaniment.

Arthur Miller: Columbia Pictures made a film called "The Life of a Salesman" which they wanted to show with the "Death of a Salesman." It was short, the brunt of which was that "the life of a salesman" was—couldn't be better: that it was a wonderful profession, that people thrived on it, and there were no problems at all.

Paul Solman: In fact, the Frederick March feature itself made Willy into a very untypical salesman—a sort of lunatic.

Arthur Miller: And, indeed, the film suffered because they tended to make him crazy. And it was a real politically influenced film, and I complained about it. But I didn't have any control over it at the time.

This photo was taken in front of Miller's farmhouse in Woodbury, Connecticut. He had just heard the news that the U.S. Court of Appeals overturned a 1957 contempt of Congress conviction against him after he refused to reveal the names of Communist writers. AP Images.

Paul Solman: You didn't have any control over the total film?

Arthur Miller: No.

Paul Solman: But what about this short?

Arthur Miller: The short I complained about and pretended I knew what I was talking about and I said, "I'll sue you for—" whatever I invented. And they—I think they showed it once or twice, but it was so dreadful that they simply withdrew it. And it's the only time that a movie company put out a picture to destroy the film that they had just made. That's how terrified people were.

A Victim of McCarthyism

Paul Solman: This was the terror of the McCarthy era when hundreds of prominent Americans were called before Congress to testify about their left-wing affiliations and name those with whom they'd associated. In 1952, two of Miller's colleagues from the original "Death of a Salesman" production—Director Elia Kazan and actor Lee J. Cobb—named names before the House Un-American Activities Committee. The 1954 movie, "On the Waterfront" was a sort of defense of their actions. When it came Miller's turn to testify before the committee, however, he refused. In fact, he didn't take the fifth, the amendment that protects Americans from self-incrimination, but the first, the right to free speech. Miller was convicted of contempt and sentenced to a year in prison. The Supreme Court later softened the blow.

Arthur Miller: They suspended the sentence but I still had to pay a $500 fine, which hurt. And so—but I must say that my thing came at the sort of—near the end of the whole fever that was not on the front pages anymore.

Paul Solman: Well, you were on the front pages!

Arthur Miller: Yeah, well, they—that's why they brung me in; it was to get back on the front page. That was the whole thing. The chairman of the House Committee on Un-American Activities told my lawyer that he'd call off the hearing if he could take a picture with Marilyn Monroe. That was what the whole thing was all about.

Paul Solman: You mean it was because you and Marilyn Monroe were married at that point?

Arthur Miller: Sure. Had we not been—I would never have been subpoenaed, in my opinion.

Paul Solman: It was during the Cold War that Miller wrote "The Crucible," a parable of the so-called McCarthy witchhunts. It also plays worldwide to this day. His "View From the Bridge" has often been revived as well, and he's been writing plays throughout, many of them critical of American culture—but none more critical nor more popular than "Death of a Salesman."

So the dog-eat-dog competitive capitalism that you see in "Death of a Salesman," are you more resigned to it; sympathetic to it?

Arthur Miller: I object to it, but formerly I thought that a socialist solution would resolve some of these problems. The only thing is, is that where we have had a socialist solution, it has raised up innumerable other problems that you stand and pause a bit before you really could go down that road.

Paul Solman: So you don't know what to do?

Arthur Miller: So—I don't know what to do.

Paul Solman: America's most famous living playwright is better known for his early than his later plays. He's been celebrated in England for decades but less so in America. Just last week [in early February 1999], however, a street in New York City's theater district was named "Arthur Miller Way."

Arthur Miller: If I could only park my car there. But I can't.

Paul Solman: But how does it feel to be—

Arthur Miller: Well, it feels great. I'm glad that in my own country, finally, this kind of recognition takes place, and I just am pleased, immensely, with the fact.

CHAPTER 2

Social Issues
in Literature

Suicide and *Death of a Salesman*

Willy Loman as a Tragic Hero

Robert A. Martin

Robert A. Martin is a professor of English at Michigan State University.

In the following selection, Martin frames his discussion of whether Willy Loman is a tragic figure by comparing ancient and modern interpretations of drama. Martin notes that ancient Greek philosopher Aristotle's ideas of drama and tragedy revolving around nobility would have clashed with Miller's modern staging of an average white-collar worker experiencing tragedy. In this analysis of Willy's suicide, Martin also debates whether or not Willy is a free agent making his own decisions and taking action or merely a pathetic figure.

What the *performance* of a play gives an audience is less a set of ideas, propositions, or abstractions about life and how to live it than what Arthur Miller has called a "felt experience," the imaginative sharing and participation in the lives and actions of imaginary characters. The performance is mythic; our sensibilities are enlivened by imaginary characters and we become engaged in their conflicts. Our thoughts and emotions are never so detached from theirs that we can remain "objective" in our feelings for them and in our judgments of them. If the play touches our humanity, we weep, or we smile; their movements move us, and our thoughts about them are kindled by our feelings toward them. Thus, we are *most* completely engaged in the play, as in any performing art, as it is being performed within a particular space and time. So it may seem, to a degree, presumptuous or meretricious to discuss those ideas of a play, of which the play touches on, without both the writer and reader having directly and immediately experienced the play itself.

Robert A. Martin, "The Nature of Tragedy in Arthur Miller's *Death of a Salesman*," *South Atlantic Review*, vol. 61, autumn 1996, pp. 97–106. Copyright © 1996 by the South Atlantic Modern Language Association. Reproduced by permission.

Yet many great plays—especially those written by Arthur Miller—are also plays that engage us directly in social, political, and moral questions, in questions that may be posed early in the plays themselves, and which continue to stimulate and engage us. Significantly, these questions may linger, or stimulate us as an audience to ask other related questions, after we have experienced the play. Not only are our feelings stirred by such drama, our ideas about the lives, the social and personal relationships of the characters and their environments, are stirred as well. So Miller does offer us a way to go back to those familiar or less familiar ideas he presents in his plays—by his near-faultless blending of the social, political, moral, and personal questions presented directly or indirectly through his characters.

Miller's great achievement as a playwright allows us to see and understand particular characters or groups of characters as possessing universal, human traits, even as we also see how their lives illuminate, by association, our own lives as individuals and as members of our larger society. In recognizing these larger concerns, we recognize as well that Miller's plays are not exclusively about individuals, but more precisely, are about humanity and human societies with all their contradictions and complications. As an audience we respond to the pointless death of one salesman; but we also respond as members of a society for whom, not the fact, but the *nature* of Willy Loman's life and death simultaneously diminishes and exalts us.

Experiencing Willy Loman

Willy Loman is not a case study to be argued or defended, but a representative character to be "felt" and "experienced." Still, in *Death of a Salesman*, we feel compelled to ask: "Who is Willy Loman?" for if we do not understand him and do not know who he is, we can hardly understand his death. We may be moved by Willy; but we also want to know what our responses are about. We have, in other words, an emotional investment in watching and hearing him with his family. How can we come to understand the nature of this experience? If Willy is a pathetic figure, do we feel this to be true—do we know this is true? Or is Willy a tragic figure? Do we feel this and know it to be true? Finally, we ask ourselves, what does this character's death mean in social terms—does it represent more than the death of one obscure salesman? To answer these questions, we must as audience and witnesses enter into our "felt experience" of Willy's life and death, and also, paradoxically, to view from a distance how his life affects our understanding of ourselves, our society, and our shared values.

For several thousand years, philosophers, those early cogent critics, have pondered the meaning of aesthetic experience. Within the realms of playwriting and the theatre, Aristotle's definition of tragedy, as described in *The Poetics*, continues to inform us of what this "felt experience" involves. According to Aristotle:

> Tragedy, then, is an imitation of an action that is serious, complete, and of a certain magnitude; in language embellished with each kind of artistic ornament, the several kinds being found in separate parts of the play; in the form of action, not of narrative; through pity and fear effecting the proper purgation of those emotions.

Aristotle Might Have Disagreed with Miller

In assessing *Death of a Salesman*, some critics have found fault with Miller's intention to portray Willy Loman as a tragic figure. Willy has been criticized for being "too little" or "too common" to meet the supposed requirement of Aristotle, i.e., that tragedy can only affect or be affected by noble beings, who are themselves of a "certain nobility or magnitude." But here, it is necessary to note two important points. First, Aristotle's *Poetics* conceives that the prime quality of tragedy is not character, but plot; and second, that Aristotle's opinion about tragedy is based only on the plays he knew—about what necessarily constitutes tragedy. Other philosophers and thinkers—including Miller—have slightly or strongly disagreed with Aristotle's extended definition. But Aristotle's definition of tragedy has retained more followers than detractors, so it is perfectly understandable that classically-oriented critics might object to Willy's qualifications as a figure of tragedy.

Eric Mottram, for one, in his essay, "Arthur Miller: The Development of a Political Dramatist in America," notes that

> If the plot is not to be simply a mocking of the non-passive man, it must show a real chance of heroism and change. This Miller fails to do.

He further argues that although Miller allows for the common man, such as Willy Loman, to be the agent, in Miller's words, who "thrusts for freedom" that as a tragic protagonist the

> common man is liable to arouse only pity as a poor fool in terror for his life unless he is allowed an understanding that his revolt is towards ends which have a specific chance of attainment.

It seems reasonable enough to raise the question, does Willy Loman really have an opportunity to develop as a free human being, or are his actions and choices those that proceed from a pitiman both of temperament and sensitivity; Willy can be moved to tears by tears, and can be moved beyond mere self-pity. Realizing that Biff loves him, Willy cries out with vibrant enthusiasm: "that boy—that boy is going to be magnificent!"

Pathetic Figure vs. Free Agent

Numerous critics have suggested that Willy's inability to understand the reality of his competitive salesman's world marks him as merely a pathetic figure, and determines, in effect, his fate. Such criticism implies that Miller fails to give Willy any chance to grow or to free himself from the siren's song of Madison Avenue. But Willy does act freely, not in destroying himself out of a sense of desperation and self-pity, but in sacrificing what is left of his life to provide a more secure future for Biff. Consequently, the small, common man has gained a kind of noble stature in acting heroically in facing death, and in a manner that few of us would have the courage to display. Willy pragmatically sees his act as one that will immediately benefit Biff through his insurance policy money, and—despite his fear—he acts out his scenario with a strong and passionate determination.

Whether Willy's suicide is seen as a noble act of self-sacrifice by his family is not the point of this play. Willy acts freely—he does *not* have to kill himself. As Miller suggests in "Tragedy and the Common Man," "the morality that the common man chooses, that distinguishes his choice from merely psychological or sociological considerations, implies first the desire and ability to *act.*" A failure to act freely—even if that free act is an act of sacrifice—conveys to the audience something more than tragedy. But Willy does act freely—and although he acts unwisely, he nevertheless acts heroically, attempting to find in action a solution that evades him in his speech and imagination.

This, however, does not argue that Willy is not, in some ways, a pathetic character. Perhaps *Death of a Salesman* has the rare quality of presenting its protagonist as both a figure of pathos *and* of heroism. If this is so, then *Death of a Salesman* is Miller's finest achievement—for it appears to artfully represent the modern dilemma specifically and generally within the American dream of materialistic success and failure. While graphically portraying the pattern of pathos in Willy Loman, which in Miller's words, means devising a character who "has fought a battle he could not possibly have won" ("Tragedy and the Common Man"), Miller also creates a

Lee J. Cobb (center) appears as Willy Loman in the original stage production of Death of a Salesman. © John Springer Collection/Corbis.

character who "is reaching for a token of immortality, a sign that he lived," and one who acts heroically on his own terms in trying to provide for his son.

Arguing Willy's Status as a Tragic Figure

And it is even conceivable that Willy's misplaced optimism, his inheritance from nineteenth-century America, is alone enough to classify him as a tragic figure. For whatever else Willy is in his penultimate moment of sacrifice—he is not pessimistic. In an interview with Phillip Gelb, Miller commented that

> Willy Loman is seeking for a kind of ecstasy in life which the machine civilization deprives people of. He is looking for his selfhood, for his immortal soul, so to speak.

It is Willy's capacity to act, to act freely, courageously, and with optimism and even ecstasy, that defines him as more of a tragic, rather than pathetic, figure. Despite our dismay at his suicide, we are nevertheless moved by Willy's desire to provide for Biff and regard him as someone who is not, finally, "in terror for his life."

In "Arthur Miller and the Idea of Modern Tragedy," M.W. Steinberg complains that

> Willy Loman does not gain "size" from the situation;... his warped values, the illusions concerning the self he projects, reflect those of his society ... he goes to his death clinging to his illusions. He is a pathetic figure, yet Miller in his essay written at this time says that there is no place for pathos in real tragedy. Pathos, he remarks, is the mode for the pessimist, suitable for the kind of struggle where a man is obviously doomed from the outset. And earlier in the essay Miller postulated that tragedy must be inherently optimistic. In Miller's view of tragedy and his expression of it in his plays, there seems to be some confusion that needs to be examined.

In *Death of a Salesman* there may be, indeed, a suggestion of a seemingly defeated character who may or may not obtain a pyrrhic victory, or even an immortal "thrust for freedom," which, according to Miller in "Tragedy and the Common Man," "is the quality in tragedy which exalts."

Steinberg is not the only critic to describe Willy's play of memory "inside his head" as that of a victim's. In *American*

Drama Since World War II, Gerald Weales notes briefly that even at the play's beginning, Willy Loman is "past the point of choice." Again, for Weales and Steinberg, Willy appears as a victim whose fate is already sealed. But if this were so, there could be no dramatic conflict possible in the play.

Clearly, Willy is a tragic, if occasionally self-contradictory, figure. That he acts unwisely in confronting Biff and in relating to his family is obvious. But his motives are well-intentioned as he struggles to achieve a victory over those forces that seem to conspire to keep his son from achieving his own dreams. Willy does not die heroically; his tragedy is that he dies blindly and alone. To argue that he does not gain size or stature from his struggle is to ignore the courage required for his sacrifice. But Willy's death serves to underscore the point that the capacity to act is considered more noble and heroic than one's limited capacity to live in harmony with a mechanistic society that eventually destroys by entropy. And although Willy is more than, as Steinberg argues, "a victim of his society"—he is a tragic victim in that he believes it is necessary to sacrifice his life in order to provide for his son. Willy has bought into the American Dream of material success and the ever elusive cult of "personality." Indeed, Willy carries with him a host of negative qualities that by themselves would make him a pathetic figure. His natural talents as a carpenter and builder have found limited outlets. His love of nature, his desire to breathe fresh air are all thwarted in his prison-like brick home in Brooklyn. Worse still, his real identity is obscured and crushed by a job that consumes his life and daily happiness.

As P.P. Sharma notes in "Search for Self-Identity in *Death of a Salesman*," Willy feels "terribly lonely and insecure," which

> is symbolically brought out in the scene when he accidentally switches on the wire recorder and, panic stricken, shouts for Howard's help. Instead of looking within himself, he looks outside to others.

As Sharma notes, Biff, unlike Willy, "gradually learns to be himself, instead of staying on as a compulsive victim."

A Dream of Dignity

Certainly, added to Willy's shortcomings are his lack of self-knowledge and successful business acumen. As an audience, we laugh at Willy's contradictions, his distorted logic, and cringe at his stubbornness. In addition, he both practices and encourages lying, cheating, stealing, violence, day-dreaming, adultery, slander, and contemptuousness. He is the butt of jokes and feels obliged to crack a salesman "right across the face" for calling him a "fat walrus." Nevertheless and notwithstanding, we feel his pathos, and are both moved by and pity his sense of obligation to Biff. Willy Loman is not merely "insecure" and a "compulsive victim," he is absolute and reveals himself as multi-dimensional. As Miller comments in the Introduction to his *Collected Plays*,

> He [Willy] has achieved a very powerful piece of knowledge, which is that he is loved by his son and has been embraced by him and forgiven.

In other words, Willy is at this point not merely a lost figure drowning in self-pity and pathos. He is a tragic figure, who attains a modern tragic stature, according to Miller, by his desire and willingness "to secure one thing—his sense of personal dignity." The knowledge that Biff loves him, despite their past differences, allows Willy to achieve a moral victory, which, for Miller, is the stuff of tragedy. Willy regains a faith in himself, just as we in the audience ponder Miller's own conception, the "belief—optimistic if you will, in the perfectibility of man" ("Tragedy and the Common Man"). The play might also have been titled *Death of a Father*.

Some critics and scholars, however, disagree with Miller's ideas on what constitutes the tragic condition and continue to view Willy as a misguided dream chaser, a character who foolishly throws his life away on the false promises of Madison Avenue, the power of money, and a desire for some imaginary self-aggrandizement. After the play is over, we may be haunted by Willy's suicide and thereby conclude that it represents an act lacking in "good faith," to borrow Jean-Paul Sartre's expression. But what elevates this play to the status of tragedy is not only Willy's self-conscious choice to sacrifice his life, but that given the nature of our society, we might also make a similar choice. If we fail to empathize with Willy, it may be as Miller suggests in the foreword to his *Theater Essays* that "we have lost the art of tragedy for want of a certain level of self-respect, finally, and are in disgrace with ourselves." And, as if to underscore his own concerns in *Death of a Salesman*, in his essay "The Family in Modern Drama," Miller has commented that:

> If, for instance, the struggle in *Death of a Salesman* were simply between father and son for recognition and forgiveness it would diminish in importance. But when it extends itself out of the family circle and into society, it broaches those questions of social status, social honor and recognition, which expand its vision and lift it out of the merely particular toward the fate of the generality of men.

Miller's Theater as a Mirror of Society

Just as Miller sees the stage as "*the* place for ideas, for philosophies, for the most intense discussions of man's fate," he also believes that we can, by contemplating dramatic tragedies, acquire that same knowledge that the tragic figure acquires "pertaining to the right way of living in the world" ("The Nature of Tragedy").

How then do Willy Loman's experiences represent those questions that social plays ask? Is there more to the idea of tragedy than transcends the struggle between father and son for forgiveness and dignity? As an audience, our "felt experience" involves our own empathetic feelings toward and about

Willy. While we may intellectually identify with him in his existential situation, we may also imaginatively feel, concerning the larger society, that someone might also be led to take "the easy way out." Not only do we pity Willy and his broken dreams, we also fear for ourselves, either at present or in the future, in which the possibility of gaining money through suicide can become a social reality—the final affirmation in a failed life. This is why Willy reflects a social pattern as well as a personal tragedy.

In his new foreword to the Methuen second edition of *The Theatre Essays*, Miller laments the decline of actors and playwrights in the theater as films and television attract them to a different medium. But he ends his lament by stating:

> Embarrassing as it may be to remind ourselves, the theatre does reflect the spirit of a people, and when it lives up to its potential it may even carry them closer to their aspirations. It is the most vulgar of the arts but it is the simplest too. . . . All you need is a human and a board to stand on and something fascinating for him to say and do. With a few right words, sometimes, he can clarify the minds of thousands, still the whirling compass needle of their souls and point it once more toward the stars. . . . Theatre is not going to die, it is as immortal as our dreaming.

The tragedy inherent in *Death of a Salesman* is no longer only an American tragedy. It is part of the universal tragedy of love, grief, despair, and betrayal that today characterizes life in most countries of the world. With "a few right words" Miller has again and again expressed in his plays the thoughts and fears of people everywhere. And occasionally he has even pointed that whirling compass needle of their souls toward the stars.

Willy Loman Is Dying
Throughout the Play

Harold Bloom

Harold Bloom is a prominent literary and cultural critic. He has written approximately thirty books, editing many more. He is the Sterling Professor of Humanities at Yale University.

In the following selection, Bloom discusses Arthur Miller's position in American theater as a social dramatist and explores Death of a Salesman *as a play of universal appeal. Referencing Miller's first successful play,* All My Sons, *Bloom draws attention to the origin of the father figure character that is later developed into Willy Loman. Bloom cites the influence on Miller of renowned writers such as Norwegian playwright Henrik Ibsen, discussing their writing in comparison with Miller's. Bloom also compares dramatic writing to literary writing. While Bloom contends that* Death of a Salesman *does not always read as a great piece of dramatic literature, onstage it comes to life, exposing the hopes and fears of an American salesman.*

Rather like [American playwright] Eugene O'Neill before him, Arthur Miller raises, at least for me, the difficult critical question as to whether there is not an element in drama that is other than literary, even contrary in value (supposed or real) to literary values, perhaps even to aesthetic values. O'Neill, a very nearly great dramatist, particularly in *The Iceman Cometh* and *Long Day's Journey into Night*, is not a good writer, except perhaps in his stage directions. Miller is by no means a bad writer, but he is scarcely an eloquent master of the language. I have just reread *All My Sons, Death of a Salesman*, and *The Crucible*, and am compelled to reflect how poorly they reread, though all of them, properly staged, are very effective dramas, and *Death of a Salesman* is considerably more than that. It ranks with *Iceman, Long Day's Journey*, [Tennessee] Williams's *A Streetcar Named Desire*, [Thornton] Wilder's *The Skin of Our Teeth* and [Edward] Albee's *The Zoo Story* as one of the half-dozen crucial American plays. Yet its literary status seems to me somewhat questionable, which returns me to the issue of what there is in drama that can survive indifferent or even poor writing.

Defending *Death of a Salesman*, despite what he admits is a sentimental glibness in its prose, Kenneth Tynan memorably observed: "But the theater is an impure craft, and *Death of a Salesman* organizes its impurities with an emotional effect unrivalled in postwar drama." The observation still seems true, long after Tynan made it, yet how unlikely a similar statement would seem if ventured about [Henrik] Ibsen, Miller's prime precursor. Do we speak of *Hedda Gabler* organizing its impurities with an unrivalled emotional effect? Why is the American drama, except for Thornton Wilder (its one great sport), addicted to an organization of impurities, a critical phrase perhaps applicable only to Theodore Dreiser, among the major American novelists? Why is it that we have brought forth *The Scarlet Letter, Moby-Dick, Adventures of Huckleberry Firm, The Portrait of a Lady, The Sun Also Rises, The Great Gatsby, As I Lay Dying, Miss Lonelyhearts, The Crying of Lot 49*, but no comparable dramas? How can a nation whose poets include [Walt] Whitman, [Emily] Dickinson, [Robert] Frost, [Wallace] Stevens, [T.S.] Elliot, Hart Crane, Elizabeth Bishop, James Merrill, and John Ashbery, among so many others of the highest aesthetic dignity—how can it offer us only O'Neill, Miller, and Williams as its strongest playwrights?

Miller as Social Dramatist

Drama at its most eminent tends not to appear either too early or too late in any national literature. The United States may be the great exception, since before O'Neill we had little better than Clyde Fitch, and our major dramas (it is to be hoped) have not yet manifested themselves. I have seen little speculation upon this matter, with the grand exception of Alvin B. Kernan, the magisterial scholarly critic of Shakespeare and of Elizabethan dramatic literature. Meditating upon American plays, in 1967, Kernan tuned his initially somber notes to hopeful ones:

> Thus with all our efforts, money, and good intentions, we have not yet achieved a theater; and we have not, I believe, because we do not see life in historic and dramatic terms. Even our greatest novelists and poets, sensitive and subtle though they are, do not think dramatically, and should not be asked to, for they express themselves and us in other forms more suited to their visions (and ours). But we have come very close at moments to having great plays, if not a great theatrical tradition. When the Tyrone family stands in its parlor looking at the mad mother holding her wedding dress and knowing that all the good will in the world cannot undo what the past has done to them; when Willy Loman, the salesman, plunges again and again into the past to search for the point where it all went irremediably wrong and cannot find any one fatal turning point; when the Antrobus family, to end on a more cheerful note, drafts stage hands from backstage to take the place of sick actors, gathers its feeble and ever-disappointed hopes, puts its miserable home together again after another in a series of unending disasters stretching from the ice age to the present; then we are very close to accepting our entanglement in the historical process and our status as actors, which may in time produce a true theater.

That time has not yet come, some thirty years later, but I think that Kernan was more right even than he knew. Our greatest novelists and poets continue not to see life in historic and dramatic terms, precisely because our literary tradition remains incurably Emersonian, and [Ralph Waldo] Emerson shrewdly dismissed both history and drama as European rather than American. An overtly anti-Emersonian poet-novelist like Robert Penn Warren does see life in historic and dramatic terms, and yet has done his best work away from the stage, despite his effort to write *All the King's Men* as a play. Our foremost novelist, Henry James, failed as a dramatist, precisely because he was more Emersonian than he knew, and turned too far inward in nuanced vision for a play to be his proper mode of representation. One hardly sees [William] Faulkner or Frost, [Ernest] Hemingway or Stevens as dramatists, though they all made their attempts. Nor would a comparison of *The Waste Land* and *The Family Reunion* be kind to Eliot's dramatic ambitions. The American literary mode, whether narrative or lyric, tends towards romance and rumination, or fantastic vision, rather than drama. Emerson, genius of the shores of America, directed us away from history, and distrusted drama as a revel. Nothing is got for nothing; Faulkner and Wallace Stevens, aesthetic light-years beyond O'Neill and Tennessee Williams, seem to mark the limits of the literary imagination in our American century. It is unfair to *All My Sons* and *Death of a Salesman* to read them with the high expectations we rightly bring to *As I Lay Dying* and *Notes Toward a Supreme Fiction*. Miller, a social dramatist, keenly aware of history, fills an authentic American need, certainly for his own time.

The Father in *All My Sons* Foreshadows Willy

All My Sons (1947), Miller's first success, retains the flavor of post–World War II America, though it is indubitably something beyond a period piece. Perhaps all of Miller's work could be titled *The Guilt of the Fathers*, which is a dark matter for a Jewish playwright, brought up to believe in the normative tradition, with its emphasis upon the virtues of the fathers. Though it is a truism to note that *All My Sons* is an Ibsenite play, the influence relation to Ibsen remains authentic, and is part of the play's meaning, in the sense that Ibsen too is one of the fathers, and shares in their guilt. Ibsen's peculiar guilt in *All My Sons* is to have appropriated most of Miller's available stock of dramatic language. The result is that this drama is admirably constructed yet not adequately expressed. It is not just that eloquence is lacking; sometimes the characters seem unable to say what they need to say if we are to be with them as we should.

Joe Keller ought to be the hero-villain of *All My Sons*, since pragmatically he certainly is a villain. But Miller is enormously fond of Joe, and so are we; he is not a good man, and yet he lives like one, in regard to family, friends, neighbors. I do not think that Miller ever is interested in Hannah Arendt's curious notion of the banality of evil. Joe is banal, and he is not evil, though his business has led him into what must be called moral idiocy, in regard to his partner, and to any world that transcends his own immediate family. Poor Joe is just not very intelligent, and it is Miller's curious gift that he can render such a man dramatically interesting. An ordinary man who wants to have a moderately good time, who wants his family never to suffer, and who lacks any imagination beyond the immediate: what is this except an authentic American Everyman? The wretched Joe simply is someone who does not know enough, indeed who scarcely knows anything at all. Nor can he learn anything. What I find least convincing in the play is Joe's moment of breaking through to a moral awareness, and a new kind of knowledge:

MOTHER: Why are you going? You'll sleep, why are you going?

KELLER: I can't sleep here. I'll feel better if I go.

MOTHER: You're so foolish. Larry was your son too, wasn't he? You know he'd never tell you to do this.

KELLER, *looking at letter in his hand*: Then what is this if it isn't telling me? Sure, he was my son. But I think to him they were all my sons. And I guess they were, I guess they were. I'll be right down. *Exits into house.*

MOTHER, *to Chris, with determination*: You're not going to take him!

CHRIS: I'm taking him.

MOTHER: It's up to you, if you tell him to stay he'll stay. Go and tell him!

CHRIS: Nobody could stop him now.

MOTHER: You'll stop him! How long will he live in prison? Are you trying to kill him?

Nothing in Joe is spiritually capable of seeing and saying: "They were all my sons. And I guess they were, I guess they were." That does not reverberate any more persuasively than Chris crying out: "There's a universe of people outside and you're responsible to it." Drama fails Miller there, or perhaps he fails drama. Joe Keller was too remote from a felt sense of reality for Miller to represent the estrangement properly, except in regard to the blindness Joe manifested towards his two sons. Miller crossed over into his one permanent achievement when he swerved from Ibsen into the marginal world of *Death of a Salesman*, where the pain is the meaning, and the meaning has a repressed but vital relationship to the normative vision that informs Jewish memory.

An American Play with Universal Appeal

The strength of *Death of a Salesman* may be puzzling, and yet is beyond dispute; the continued vitality of the play cannot be questioned. Whether it has the aesthetic dignity of tragedy is not clear, but no other American play is worthier of the term, so far. I myself resist the drama each time I reread it, because it seems that its language will not hold me, and then I see it played on stage, and I yield to it. Miller has caught an American kind of suffering that is also a universal mode of pain, quite possibly because his hidden paradigm for his American tragedy is an ancient Jewish one. Willy Loman is hardly a biblical figure, and he is not supposed to be Jewish, yet something crucial in him is Jewish, and the play does belong to that undefined entity we can call Jewish literature, just as [playwright Harold] Pinter's *The Caretaker* rather surprisingly does. The only meaning of Willy Loman is the pain he suffers, and the pain his fate causes us to suffer. His tragedy makes sense only in the Freudian world of repression, which happens also to be the world of normative Jewish memory. It is a world in which everything has already happened, in which there never can be anything new again, because there is a total sense or meaningfulness in everything, which is to say, in which everything hurts.

That cosmos informed by Jewish memory is the secret strength or permanent coherence of *Death of a Salesman*, and accounts for its ability to withstand the shrewd critique of Eric Bentley, who found that the genres of tragedy and of social drama destroyed one another here. Miller's passionate insistence upon tragedy is partly justified by Willy's perpetual sense of being in exile. Commenting on his play, Miller wrote that: "The truly valueless man, a man without ideals, is always perfectly at home anywhere." But Willy, in his own small but valid way, has his own version of the Nietzschean "desire to be elsewhere, the desire to be different," and it does reduce to a Jewish version. Doubtless, as [literary critic] Mary McCarthy first noted, Willy "could not be Jewish because he had to be American." Nearly forty years later, that distinction is pragmatically blurred, and we can wonder if the play might be stronger if Willy were more overtly Jewish.

We first hear Willy say: "It's all right. I came back." His last utterance is the mere repetition of the desperately hushing syllable: "Shhh!" just before he rushes out to destroy himself. A survivor who no longer desires to survive is something other than a tragic figure. Willy, hardly a figure of capable imagination, nevertheless is a representation of terrible pathos. Can we define precisely what that pathos is?

Probably the most famous speech in *Death of a Salesman* is Linda's pre-elegy for her husband, of whom she is soon to remark: "A small man can be just as exhausted as a great man." The plangency of Linda's lament has a universal poignance, even if we wince at its naked design upon us:

> Willy Loman never made a lot of money. His name was never in the paper. He's not the finest character that ever lived. But he's a human being, and a terrible thing is happening to him. So attention must be paid. He's not to be allowed to fall into his grave like an old dog. Attention, attention must be finally paid to such a person.

Behind this is Miller's belated insistence "that everyone knew Willy Loman," which is a flawed emphasis on Miller's part, since he first thought of calling the play *The Inside of His Head*, and Willy already lives in a phantasmagoria when the drama opens. You cannot know a man half lost in the American dream, a man who is unable to tell past from present. Perhaps the play should have been called *The Dying of a Salesman*, because Willy is dying throughout. That is the pathos of Linda's passionate injunction that attention must be finally paid to such a person, a human being to whom a terrible thing is happening. Nothing finds Willy anymore; everything loses him. He is a man upon whom the sun has gone down, to appropriate a great phrase from [poet] Ezra Pound. But have we defined as yet what is particular about his pathos?

I think not. Miller, a passionate moralist, all but rabbinical in his ethical vision, insists upon giving us Willy's, and his sons', sexual infidelities as synecdoches of the failure of Willy's vision of reality. Presumably, Willy's sense of failure, his belief that he has no right to his wife, despite Linda's love for him, is what motivates Willy's deceptions, and those of his sons after him. Yet Willy is not destroyed by his sense of failure. Miller may be a better interpreter of Miller than he is a dramatist. I find it wholly persuasive that Willy is destroyed by love, by his sudden awareness that his son Biff truly loves him. Miller beautifully comments that Willy resolves to die when "he is given his existence . . . his fatherhood, for which he has always striven and which until now he could not achieve." That evidently is the precise and terrible pathos of Willy's character and of his fate. He is a good man, who wants only to earn and to deserve the love of his wife and of his sons. He is self-slain, not by the salesman's dream of America, but by the universal desire to be loved by one's own, and to be loved beyond what one believes one deserves. Miller is not one of the masters of metaphor, but in *Death of a Salesman* he memorably achieves a pathos that none of us would be wise to dismiss.

The Ambiguity of Biff's Feelings for Willy

H.C. Phelps

In the following selection, H.C. Phelps takes a focused look at the relationship between Willy Loman and his son Biff. Biff's anger toward his father becomes sadness and a cry for understanding in a climactic scene between the two of them, their final exchange of words. At the conclusion of the scene, Willy is buoyed by the belief that Biff loves him, asking for reassurance from the rest of the family. Phelps analyzes Willy's suicide in terms of his relationship and last words with his son, asserting that it is unclear whether Biff really does love his father.

Curiously, most critics seem to accept at face value the assumption that at the conclusion of Arthur Miller's classic drama *Death of a Salesman*, Willy Loman determines to commit suicide because his older son Biff has at last openly and unequivocally declared his "love" for his father. Yet a close examination of this crucial scene and the subsequent Requiem reveals a far greater degree of ambiguity than has been acknowledged.

Biff Expresses Concern to His Father

Though Willy has obviously contemplated suicide for a long time, he only makes his final, irrevocable decision after the play has reached its undoubted emotional climax, Biff's dramatic declaration to his father: "Pop, I'm nothing! I'm nothing, Pop. Can't you understand that? There's no spite in it anymore. I'm just what I am, that's all." Following this outburst, Biff physically collapses in his father's arms, and Miller

H. C. Phelps, "Miller's *Death of a Salesman.*" *Explicator*, vol. 53, summer 1995, pp. 239–240. Copyright © 1995 by Helen Dwight Reid Educational Foundation. Reproduced with permission of the Helen Dwight Reid Educational Foundation, published by Heldref Publications, 1319 18th Street, NW, Washington, DC 20036-1802.

Miller walks past the theater sign advertising the original production of Death of a Salesman *in 1949.* AP Images.

carefully comments in his stage direction: "Biff's fury has spent itself, and he breaks down, sobbing, holding on to Willy, who dumbly fumbles for Biff's face." The son's final words to his father in the play are simply: "I'll go in the morning. Put him—put him to bed."

Concern Is Interpreted as Love

At best, this statement can only be regarded as a tepid and ambiguous expression of concern. Yet Willy's immediate reaction to it is to conclude: "Biff—he likes me!" To which Linda and Happy quickly respond with enthusiastic reinforcement: "He loves you, Willy!" and "Always did, Pop." Their reaction suggests that Biff's feelings are obvious. However, Linda and Happy are repeatedly shown to be among the most deluded, obtuse, and mendacious characters in the play. Earlier, each had made equally enthusiastic and reinforcing, but dangerously inaccurate—comments on the supposed affection of Bill Oliver, Biff's former boss, for his departed employee. When Biff outlined his plan to persuade Oliver to "stake" him to a business venture, he insisted: "He did like me. Always liked me." Linda immediately exclaimed: "He loved you." Earlier, Happy had responded to the plan in a similar fashion: "I bet he'd back you. "Cause he thought highly of you, Biff." Yet Oliver, when Biff finally sees him in his office, doesn't "remember who [Biff] was or anything."

The Ambiguity of Biff's Feelings for Willy

Even the choice of words of Linda's and Happy's comments in the scene with Willy seems deliberately to echo their earlier remarks, as if Miller is intentionally undermining their credibility in this scene. And if their reactions are as erroneous as they had been earlier with Oliver, it casts Willy's subsequent suicide into a new light. For it is primarily due to their insistence on Biff's love for his father, not to any explicit comment by his son, that Willy decides to take his own life to provide Biff with insurance money for a fresh start.

If Biff does indeed not love his father, Willy's suicide must be regarded as just the last in the series of futile, misguided gestures that made up his life. Biff's awareness of this fact, then, would go far to explain his puzzling tension and bitterness at the Requiem, where he argues sullenly with Happy,

Charley, and Linda. For perhaps he realizes that to make plain the sad futility of Willy's act would be to rob the ceremony of what little dignity it possesses. Therefore, he remains virtually silent as the other mourners express their eloquent, if contradictory, judgments on Willy's life, insisting only that his father "had the wrong dreams" and "never knew who he was." If the belief that Biff "loves" Willy is only the final, most tragic false perception in a play permeated by such uncertainty, the son's silence on this critical point is both understandable and justified.

Many Factors Led to Willy's Suicide

Sighle Kennedy

Sighle Kennedy is a scholar specializing in the works of author and playwright Samuel Beckett.

In the following essay, Kennedy asks, "Who killed the salesman?" Instead of pointing to a single cause for Willy Loman's suicide, Kennedy discerns many factors. The play not only asks who or what killed Willy, but also what might have become of Willy had he lived and what will become of his son Biff. Kennedy acknowledges that the play ends with unanswered questions but suggests that Arthur Miller has admirably spurred audiences to seek the answers for themselves.

It was on the night of February 10, 1949, that Willy Loman first rushed off a Broadway stage. As his wife cried out after him in fear, "Willy? Willy, answer me!" the theater was filled with the roar of a car starting and speeding away. Then a crash. And the audience knew that Salesman Willy Loman had wrecked the car and killed himself to leave his family $20,000 in insurance money. No one on the stage tried to deny the fact. Willy Loman—the hero of Arthur Miller's play, *Death of a Salesman*—was a suicide.

To the thousand people who filed out of the theater that night, and to the 400,000 people who have seen the play since then in New York City alone [as of about 1950] the vision of Willy Loman has been (let the critics speak for the rest) "overpowering," "shattering," "unforgettable." It has made most of them feel, not "there but for the grace of God go I," but, "there go I right now unless the grace of God (or some agnostic substitute) suddenly acts to stop me."

Sighle Kennedy, "Who Killed the Salesman?" *Catholic World*, vol. 170, May 1970, pp. 110–116. Copyright © 1970 by Sighle Kennedy. Paulist Press, Inc., New York/Mahwah, NJ. Reprinted by permission of Paulist Press, Inc. www.paulistpress.com.

The question of whether or not *Death of a Salesman* is a great dramatic structure, or whether or not its writing is splendid or only roughly adequate, can hold but secondary importance in any discussion of the play. Above them one fact shines! Willy Loman, egotistical, greedy, affectionate, lonely, has risen up as a Modern Everyman.

But the very way in which Willy speaks so immediately to so many people has brought his problems into sharp and varied scrutiny. The play is now being given not only by four companies throughout the U.S. but by groups in England, Switzerland, Italy, France, Germany, Greece, Argentina, Israel, and by another four groups in Scandinavia. It speaks not only to, and for the problem of, an American audience but to countries whose insecurity is even more obvious than that of the U.S. represented by Willy—countries which often look toward the U.S. as an easy and automatic way out of their troubles. To them, as to Americans, the self-destroyed Willy rises up in warning.

Willy as a Helpless Little Man

So powerfully projected and personally received has been this story of Willy Loman that a not-surprising doubt has risen up about it. People see in it an accurate picture of their own mental stresses and feel defensive about Willy. Many of them wonder: was Willy really responsible for his death, or was he, as Luke Carroll in the *Herald Tribune* put it, "a pathetic little man caught in an undertow that's much too strong for him?"

Gene Lockhart, who plays the part of Willy in New York [in 1949–50], has been impressed by the earnest tone of his fan letters and visitors. "So many of them," he commented when interviewed for this article, "begin by saying, 'You know, the play made me think.'"

Was Willy the victim of brute economics? Or of an unbounded, irrational desire for success? Or of the thoughtless ingratitude of his sons? These questions and many others have remained with the *Salesman*'s audience long after the final curtain has gone down.

Perhaps the largest single group that thinks of Willy as a helpless "little man" is made up of those who see economics as the all-powerful factor in the play. They make the most of the epitaph spoken by Willy's friend, Charley: "Nobody dast blame this man. . . . For a Salesman, there is no rock bottom to the life. He don't put a bolt to a nut, he don't tell you the law or give you medicine. . . . A salesman is got to dream, boy. It comes with the territory." The territory, they say (and have said all along), is to blame. Willy had no chance against the capitalistic system.

The other half of the group is at the opposite extreme of belief. They also feel that economics is the determining power in the play, but they believe that Miller, in criticizing "the territory," is trying to undermine democracy. "It's not true that the *Death of a Salesman* gives a true picture," said one indignant businessman at a Chamber of Commerce Executive's meeting in St. Louis. "The professional salesman has . . . a life built upon the foundation stone of attitude, knowledge, integrity and industry."

Such a group contends that Miller has stacked the cards against Willy and used his single tragedy to point an unjustifiable finger at salesmanship itself. If Willy died, they say in effect, Arthur Miller killed him.

"A Salesman Is Everybody"

But most people who saw the play or read it (200,000 copies have been distributed through the Book-of-the-Month Club alone) do not feel that either of these exclusively economic views is sufficient to explain Willy's death.

A more percipient businessman speaking through *Fortune* magazine, the very Valhalla of salesmanship, said, "Willy represents any man whose illusions have made him incapable of dealing realistically with everyday life." The article was entitled "A Salesman Is Everybody."

If one hears out the play with an open mind, it is hard not to agree with this last opinion. Far from painting a one-sided economic picture, Miller is almost painfully scrupulous in showing that Willy's tragedy must not be set at the door of his particular type of work (symbolic though that surely is). Willy's braggadocio, his confidence that he and his sons, by divine right of personality, are above the laws that bind ordinary men, put his acts in the realm of universal moral censure—not in the cubby-hole of an ideology.

Even more specific proof of the play's lack of bias is the fact that Charley, Willy's neighbor and sincere friend, is a successful businessman. Charley not only lends Willy money, but constantly tries to help him out of his self-pity, to calm the frustrated rages which finally lead him to madness.

When Willy is fired by the ungrateful son of his old boss, Charley offers him a job. Willy, from vanity, will not accept. The only reason that Willy can make his final grand gesture of leaving insurance money is because Charley has been paying the last installments. Grudgingly, Willy says: "Charley, you're the only friend I've got. Isn't that a remarkable thing?" Charley takes no credit for his good neighbor policy, only wryly remarks at one point: "You sneeze in here, and in my house hats blow off."

With Charley living next door, economics can hardly be termed the nemesis of Willy's life. His failure as a man is the cause, rather than the effect, of his economic failure.

But the working of Willy's mind, confronted shockingly as it is with life, death and the terrible insecurities that grow up between the two, has also fascinated psychologists—professional and amateur alike. It is interesting to note that their suggestions, in true detective-story fashion, implicate almost every other member of the cast.

Linda Loman Is Above Suspicion

The one character who can be immediately absolved from suspicion is Linda, Willy's wife. In spite of the fact that Willy, with all his bragging, has barely made enough to support his family, and although he treats her with increasing rudeness as his discontent drives him more and more inside himself, her goodness never fails. She loves and explains Willy without ever being able to reach him. Her speeches are touching, but rather harrowing, in their helplessness: "I search and search and I search, and I can't understand," she says, ". . . I live from day to day."

Her one positive action is to cry out for help, and her voice does reach her two careless sons—"Attention," she insists, "attention must be finally paid to such a man. He's a human being and a terrible thing is happening to him. He's not to be allowed to fall into his grave like an old dog."

The Failures of Willy's Sons

The sons, Biff and Happy, inherit their father's worst qualities, and the various tensions between them leave plenty of scope for all sorts of analysis. Biff, the older and more gifted in every way, at first seems destined to fulfill all his father's dreams. In school he was handsome, popular, a great athlete, a leader. Willy idolizes his son and fills him with contempt for humdrum responsibilities.

When Biff steals school footballs, Willy laughingly calls it "initiative." When he bullies his classmates and cheats at exams, his father encourages him, thinks him "a fearless character." But when, in a crucial examination, Biff runs up against a professor he can neither bluff nor cheat, he learns that his father has failed him doubly. He follows Willy to Boston to ask for help—and finds him in a hotel with a woman. Suddenly he senses, rather than sees, the complete falsehood of his father's life—and the falsehood of the life he himself has been brought up to lead.

Hopelessly indulged, however, as he is, he has no values now to give him balance. Even Willy's shame and contrition ("She's nothing to me, Biff, I was just lonely, terribly lonely.") merely harden him. At the final action of the play Biff is thirty-four, still unsettled. He is satisfied only when he is working on a farm, but keeps drifting because of a recurrent dread of "not getting anywhere."

Biff's failure is one of the things that Willy will not let himself face. "It's all spite . . . spite," he tries to believe. Linda never knows the reason for the break between father and son but she knows that his sons represent the hardest part of Willy's punishment. "I tell you," she pleads with them, "he put his whole life into you and you've turned your backs on him. . . . Biff, his life is in your hands."

Biff's sympathy for his father's suffering finally does overcome his resentment. He makes a last desperate attempt to open Willy's eyes to the truth—to make him understand that neither of them can achieve the success for which Willy has hoped—"Pop, I'm nothing. . . . Can't you understand that? Will you take that phony dream and burn it before something happens?"

But Willy's warped mind can no longer follow any bent but its own. He only senses the affection in Biff's voice and this knowledge leads ironically to a resurrection of all his flashiest ambitions. "That boy," he cries out pathetically, "that boy is going to be magnificent! Can you imagine that magnificence with twenty thousand dollars in his pocket? When the mail comes he'll be ahead of Bernard again!" (Bernard is Charley's lawyer-son, of whose success Willy cannot help but be jealous.) And Willy rushes off to death for money that nobody wants—money that helps nobody.

Happy, the second son, represents no such dramatic struggle. He is a marked-down version of his father, with not even a grand dream to cover his grossness. His only redeeming aspect is an easy-going fondness for his family.

One psychiatrist (Dr. Daniel Schneider, writing in *Theatre Arts*) has interpreted the whole play as a dream of Happy's to get revenge on his father for paying more attention to Biff than to him—resolving the play into death by compound Oedipus complex!

Willy Is Guided by the Memory of His Brother

The last important personage—and the most baleful—is a man who has been dead fifteen years. Ben, Willy's older brother, is a symbol of the ruthless success Willy has never reached. "There was the only man I ever met," Willy says, "who knew all the answers." He has treasured up the memory of Ben until it is more real to him than any of the people in his life.

The figure of Ben materializes again and again on the stage and Willy savors his favorite brag: "When I was seventeen I walked into the jungle and when I was twenty-one I walked out. And, by God, I was rich."

"Rich," echoes Willy, thinking of his sons, "that's just the spirit I want to imbue them with! To walk into a jungle!" Willy has absorbed the spirit of Ben's jungle tactics, "Never fight fair with a stranger, boy. You'll never get out of the jungle that way." He comes to think of life, not as a mutually helpful state, but as a jungle, "dark but full of diamonds."

One very significant scene shows the struggle of Willy between two worlds: the destructive dream of Ben and the real world of Charley who is trying to distract him by asking about his work, by playing casino. In spite of all Charley's efforts, Willy's mind keeps slipping back to Ben, whom he sees as clearly as he does Charley. He keeps trying to talk to both at once, getting more and more confused.

Suddenly, to cover up his mistakes, Willy accuses Charley of cheating at the cards and sends him home hurt and baffled. The voice of Ben speaks out more and more clearly: "Twenty thousand—that *is* something one can feel with the hand, it is there.... It does take a great kind of man to crack the jungle.... One must go in to fetch a diamond out." Ben's words and example—grown to an obsession—directly lure Willy to his death.

Suicide as the Sum of All

The very multiplicity of problems which confront Willy must put us on our guard against placing too much stress on any one of them. Yet if no single cause compelled Willy's suicide, was it perhaps the sum of all of them? Two facts seem to answer this last question. This first is the action of the play itself. Miller has shown Willy, through the years, letting his vanity and pretensions undermine his sense of right and wrong. He repays those who try to help him only with contempt. At the end of the play he has swollen to the dreadful traditional figure of tragedy—destroyed by a single cancerous fault.

The second fact (if this first is not sufficient) is the testimony of Miller himself. In several very earnest articles he has made clear his belief that a play based on pathos—"pity for a helpless victim"—presents an essentially false view of life. The contrast to pathos is tragedy, he says, "which must illustrate a principle of life.... Our lack of tragedy may be partially accounted for by the turn which modern literature has taken toward the purely psychiatric view of life, or the purely sociological.

"If all our miseries, our indignities are born and bred within our minds, then all action, let alone the heroic action is obviously impossible. And if society alone is responsible for the cramping of our lives, then the protagonist must be so pure and faultless as to force us to deny his validity as a character. From neither of these views can tragedy derive, simply because neither represents a balanced concept of life."

In theory as in dramatic practice, Miller shows the same brave and deliberate effort to meet problems "in head-on collision"—and take the consequences. His stated aims not only show him well worth a thoughtful hearing, but they set a very high standard for judgment of his work. He believes that "tragedy brings not only sadness . . . but knowledge. What sort of knowledge? In the largest sense of the word it is knowledge pertaining to the right way of living in the world. . . . Tragedy . . . makes us aware of what the character might have been. But to say . . . what a man might have been requires of the author a soundly based, completely believed vision of man's greatest possibilities."

Does *Death of a Salesman* "make us aware of what Willy Loman might have been"? Another statement of Miller's, this one marking the play's first birthday on Broadway, supplies a clue to the answer. He notes several disappointments—"one above all. I am sorry the self-realization of the older son, Biff, is not a weightier counterbalance of Willy's disaster."

Willy Loman and What "Might Have Been"

Certainly, Biff, if anyone, should be the one to demonstrate what Willy "might have been" and what the "right way of living" is which might have saved him. What does Biff say? He says—"I'm nothing"—at least the beginning of wisdom. He further implies that his value will consist in doing the outdoor physical work he is best fitted for.

At Willy's grave, he thinks of what his father has thrown away—"There were a lot of nice days. When he'd come from a trip; or on Sundays, making the stoop. . . . You know something, Charley, there's more of him in that front stoop than in all the sales he ever made." Charley agrees: "He was a happy man with a batch of cement."

True and touching as these reminiscences are, they seem on another level entirely from the dreams, the furies ("all, all, wrong") that are shown at work in Willy. These driving forces, which all of us have felt pressing on our lives from one direction or another indeed seem to call for a "weightier counter-balance" than these words of Biff provide.

From the character of Charley, too, we might expect some statement of vision, but Charley never seems able to illumine the principle that underlies his good deeds. This lack appears in terrible relief when, after being fired, the disillusioned Willy says to him: "After all the highways, and the trains, and the appointments, and the years, you end up worth more dead than alive." Charlie's answer is not only negative, but a double negative. "Willy," he says, "nobody's worth nothing dead." How very little light that sheds on the right way of living!

At Willy's grave Charley shows more insight. When Linda wonders that Willy should choose death when "he only needed a little salary," Charley replies: "No man only needs a little salary." (A reply which manages to strike at the root of all economic materialisms.)

What might Willy Loman have been? What can Biff Loman become? These great possibilities are left for each person in the audience to answer for himself. Brooks Atkinson noted in his review: "Miller has no moral precepts to offer. . . . He is full of pity, but he brings no piety." Taken in the largest sense, as Miller would want it to be, this can only indicate a grave defect in his play's total vision. Even the "self-realization" of Biff turns inevitably into another question. If no man's satisfaction can be found in a "little salary," can it really rest ultimately in a little "cement"?

In spite of the fact, however, that *Death of a Salesman* ends so, with a question rather than an answer, Arthur Miller has performed in its creation an act of truly heroic stature. His far-reaching, sympathetic and insistent formulation of Willy's question has made millions of Willys in his audience care deeply about the answer—the best way, surely, of spurring them to find it.

Willy Loman Had the Wrong Dreams

Joseph L. Badaracco Jr.

Joseph L. Badaracco Jr. is the John Shad Professor of Business Ethics at Harvard Business School and senior associate dean and chair of the Master's in Business Administration Program. His book Questions of Character: Illuminating the Heart of Leadership Through Literature, *from which the following selection was taken, analyzes literary works for insights on present-day business ethics.*

In the following selection, Joseph L. Badaracco Jr. questions the American Dream that captivates Willy Loman. Badaracco examines personal character, ethics, and their connections with one's aspirations within the context of Death of a Salesman. *The author explains that Willy's obsession with fulfilling his dreams, but taking no joy or interest in working toward them, leads to his destruction. Furthermore, Badaracco asserts that Willy had the wrong dreams—in large part because they are not based on a realistic assessment of his life and his abilities.*

A good dream is a crucial inner resource for leaders. Great businesses, great ideas, and great accomplishments usually originate in an individual's deepest aspirations. A compelling image—of a better world and a best life for themselves—impels them forward through obstacles and hardships and engages the aspirations and dreams of others. David Lilienthal, who ran the Tennessee Valley Authority for twenty years and then headed the Atomic Energy Commission, once wrote, "The managerial life is the broadest, the most demanding, and by all odds the most comprehensive and subtle of all human

Joseph L. Badaracco Jr., "Do I Have a Good Dream?" *Questions of Character: Illuminating the Heart of Leadership Through Literature*, Boston: Harvard Business School Press, 2006. pp. 11–29.

activities." Its aim, he believed, was "to lead and move and bring out the latent capabilities—and dreams—of other human beings."

When a leader's dream goes wrong, the consequences—for leaders, families, and organizations—can be devastating. Arthur Miller's play *The Death of a Salesman* puts two propositions about dreams in front of us. One is thought-provoking, the other deeply disturbing. The challenging idea is that we are all creatures of our dreams. Some of us have a single, dominant dream; others have a multitude of hopes and aspirations. Some of our dreams are clear, others blurry or confused or unconscious. But Miller strongly suggests that dreams drive all of us. The disconcerting proposition is that the wrong dreams are slow-acting poisons. They eat away at a person's closest and most important relationships and destroy the dreamer as well—steadily, quietly, insidiously. And, until it's too late, we may not even know what is happening.

Near the end of the play, in one of the saddest scenes in American drama, we see the toxic power of the wrong dreams. The setting is the Loman family's kitchen, a simple, bare, forlorn room. Willy Loman is arguing fiercely with his son Biff. The two seem moments away from swinging at each other. Willy's wife, Linda, is watching fearfully.

Willy and Biff were once very close, back when Biff was in high school. Willy loved his sons and lived for them. He was a traveling salesman, on the road every week, and the frequent separations intensified Willy's relationships with his sons. Biff admired his father deeply, and Willy had hoped Biff would someday be a "leader of men." Now, roughly fifteen years later, Biff says he is leaving his family forever. He says, "Dad, you're never going to see what I am, so what's the use of arguing. If I strike oil, I'll send you a check. Meantime forget I'm alive." Biff offers to shake his father's hand before leaving, but Willy refuses.

In many discussions of this scene, a room can become very still—because most people have lived through similar experiences. Some involve their own parents or children, the breakups of marriages and long-time friendships, or bitter clashes between business partners or longtime coworkers. Perhaps nothing is forever, but we still look back and wonder why some relationships began with such promise and turn out so badly.

What drove the terrible wedge between Willy and Biff? Throughout the play, Arthur Miller points toward an answer: Willy's dreams for his career and his family. This disturbing conclusion raises hard questions for men and women in positions of leadership: What was wrong with Willy's dream? Do my dreams resemble his? Am I in similar danger? How do I judge the caliber of my aspirations for life and work?

The Life of a Salesman

When we meet Willy at the beginning of the play, he is worn-out, sad, and confused. His mind jerks rapidly between past and present, and both seem real to him. We learn that his father was an itinerant flute maker who died when Willy was young. He says nothing about his mother, and has a shadowy older brother, named Ben, who apparently made a lot of money in the African diamond business.

Willy lives in two spheres. One is the family he sees on weekends, when he returns from his week-long sales trips to New England. In flashbacks, we see how badly his family missed him. Willy's other world is work, which is lonely and often frustrating because Willy is a poor salesman and an unattractive person. While his two sons were growing up, these worlds were separate, so Willy could pretend to his sons that he was a stellar salesman, who knew the mayor in every city he visited. His wife Linda knew the truth, of course, because she paid the bills, and Willy's wages barely covered them.

Two things sustain Willy on the long slog of a road man. One is hard work. Willy knows that other salesmen rack up bigger commissions with less effort and that some of his customers laugh at him behind his back, but he perseveres, year after year. The other consolation is his dreams. He hopes that he will someday catch a break and be "big." When that hope fades, Willy puts all his emotional chips on Biff.

Eventually, Willy's two worlds collide. Biff had been a star quarterback in high school and won a college scholarship, but he had soon jeopardized it by failing a math course. Because Biff believed his father could work miracles, he traveled to Boston, where Willy was working, and went to his hotel room—unannounced. Biff knocked on the door, but Willy wouldn't let him in. Then, moments later, Biff discovered that his revered father was having an affair.

Willy first lied and then said honestly, "She's nothing to me, Biff. But I was lonely, I was terribly lonely." Biff called his father a liar and a "phony little fake" and left. He didn't return home for a month, refused to take a summer school math course, and never went to college. Biff spent the next decade as a drifter, working on ranches and farms, which he loved. From time to time, he went home, but soon started fighting with Willy and stormed out. Biff hates Willy for cheating on his mother and for blowing him full of hot air. Willy oscillates between saying Biff is lazy and spiteful and hoping that, with the right break, he will still make it big.

By the end of the play, Willy has been fired and had several car accidents, his mind is breaking up, and he has hidden a small rubber tube near the furnace in the basement in case he decides to kill himself—which is what he finally does. He crashes his car and dies, hoping the insurance proceeds will enable Biff to fulfill Willy's dreams for him.

Willy Loman and Everyone Else

At first glance, Willy is easy to pity and hard to like. He can be petty, mean, and prideful. In some of his flashbacks, we see him training his sons in mediocre values. A natural reaction is to view him as a moral and psychological oddity, someone so different from the rest of us that we can't learn anything from him. But audiences and readers don't see Willy this way. *Death of a Salesman* is among the most popular plays of the last century, and it continues to move audiences deeply. When the play was revived on Broadway in 1999 for its fiftieth anniversary, Brian Dennehy, who played Willy, said, "I see extremely sophisticated, very successful New Yorkers with absolutely no questions at all about who they are, how far they've come, and how right their lives are. I see them dissolve in tears, their shoulders shaking, ready to just go home."

If we look past Willy's manifest failings, what do we find? The short answer is, someone like ourselves or people we know. The conventional wisdom about *Death of a Salesman* is that Willy embraced a corrupt version of the American dream that defines success as money, status, and celebrity. The play was written in the late 1940s, and critics of capitalism see it as a brilliant indictment of the modern American economy: one writer called it "a time bomb expertly placed under the edifice of Americanism."

But this view treats Willy as an anticapitalist icon and not a human being. In fact, Miller considered calling the play *The Inside of His Head* to emphasize Willy's emotional and psychological life, and Miller thought Willy wasn't much different from most of us. He later wrote that Willy Loman was trying to fulfill "a need greater than hunger or sex or thirst, a need to leave a thumbprint somewhere on the world . . . knowing that one has carefully inscribed one's name on a cake of ice on a hot July day."

Willy works in the middle of a large organization that doesn't care much about him. He desperately wants to be a good parent. At several points, we see him giving sound, realistic advice to his sons, and the unfortunate ideals of success he tries to pass along are those of the society around him. More important, while his sons are growing up, Willy sets a strong, personal example of hard work and dedication to his job, and he provides his family with a solid, middle-class standard of living, a genuine accomplishment during the Great Depression.

Even Willy's failings have soft edges. He feels very guilty about his affair and what it did to Biff. This doesn't excuse him, but remorse about misdeeds is a sign of sound character. Willy's life on the road is hard and lonely, so we can understand why he inflates his accomplishments. Willy's neighbor and friend, Charley, is a businessman who understands what Willy is up against. At Willy's graveside, Charley tells Biff:

> Nobody dast blame this man. You don't understand: Willy was a salesman. And for a salesman, there is no rock bottom to the life. He don't put a bolt to a nut, he don't tell you law or give you medicine. He's a man way out there in the blue, riding on a smile and a shoeshine. And when they start not smiling back—that's an earthquake. And then you get yourself a couple of spots on your hat, and you're finished. Nobody dast blame this man. A salesman is got to dream, boy. It comes with the territory.

It is also hard to be critical about Willy's aspirations for his career. When he was young, Willy met Dave Singleman, an eighty-four-year-old salesman. Singleman no longer traveled but worked from a nice hotel room, where he sat in green velvet slippers and called buyers on the phone. When Singleman died, hundreds of salesmen and buyers attended the funeral, which Willy calls "the death of a salesman." Willy later says there is nothing better than to "be remembered and loved and helped by so many different people." In other words, the Willy Loman who went into sales wasn't a money-grubber or obsessed with making it big.

Questions of Character

So what went wrong? What ruined Willy's hopes for himself and his family? Arthur Miller wrote a play, not a moral treatise or a self-improvement book, so he doesn't provide rules for distinguishing good dreams from bad ones. Hence, the best way to learn from Willy Loman's tragedy is to think hard about the questions it raises. For leaders, four questions are particularly important.

Am I Dreaming with My Eyes Wide Open?

This first question sounds odd. It originates with the British archeologist, adventurer, and military strategist T.E. Lawrence—better known as "Lawrence of Arabia" for his daring role in helping the Arabs fight the Turks during World War I. In his memoirs, Lawrence writes, "All men dream: but not equally. Those who dream by night in the dusty recesses of their minds wake in the day to find that it was vanity; but the dreamers of the day are dangerous men, for they may act their dream with open eyes, to make it possible."

At first glance, it seems wrong to criticize some dreams for being unrealistic or mere "vanity." Aren't dreams supposed to be unrealistic? The great, inspiring achievements of history all looked impossible at some point. A realistic David would have run from Goliath. The American revolutionaries, and their African and Asian counterparts two centuries later, would never have challenged the British Empire. A handful of American civil rights leaders in the 1950s would never have taken on the legacy of two hundred years of slavery and another century of near-apartheid. Realism too easily leads to patience, delay, or even passivity and defeat. Surely our reach should exceed our grasp.

On the other hand, during the Internet bubble, billions of dollars were wasted on unrealistic business dreams. Some were scams, but most were clever but deeply unrealistic concepts advocated by honest men and women. All too often, dreams and vision were confused with real entrepreneurship, which a leading scholar has defined, in pragmatic and unromantic terms, as "the pursuit of opportunity beyond the resources you control." Willy Loman's story, like many other works of serious fiction, shows the dangers of dreams that are easily conjured up at night. These stories also show that it is realism—about the world and about one's self—that separates dreams from delusions.

In many ways, Linda is the real leader of the Loman family. She understands and even shares Willy's hopes and longings, but she dreams with her eyes wide open. At one point, for example, Willy recalls a scene that probably occurred on countess Friday afternoons. He had just returned from a week on the road and told Linda he had sold twelve hundred gross in Boston and Providence. Linda got out a pencil and paper, calculated his commission, and said, "Two hundred—my God! Two hundred and twelve dollars!" Willy then started backing off, saying he really hadn't added up his total sales, and that he "woulda broke records" if some stores hadn't been closed for inventory. Linda eventually calculated that his commission was about seventy dollars and told Willy that this was "very good."

Linda, the realist, walked a fine line. She didn't want to demoralize Willy at the end of a long, hard, and disappointing week; she knew he would need confidence in himself when he hit the road again on Monday morning, and she understood and shared his dream of success. But Linda wouldn't play the game of "I woulda broke records." She put the numbers in front of Willy and explained, in simple, factual terms, what they owed for car repairs, patches to the roof, payments on the vacuum cleaner, and the like. When Willy reacted by railing at the manufacturers for cheating him with defective products, Linda just came back to the facts. Eventually, they concluded, as they probably did on so many Friday afternoons, that their finances were really tight.

Throughout the play, Linda faces the same struggle: helping Willy accept who he really is while maintaining the self-assurance and hope he needs. Instead of doing what Willy does—peeking at reality and then looking away—she tells

Fans gather to watch the stars arrive at the premiere of Death of a Salesman *in Beverly Hills in 1952.* Slim Aarons/Hulton Archive/Getty Images.

him, "But you're doing wonderful, dear. You're making seventy to a hundred dollars a week." Linda is supportive, encouraging, and realistic. Despite Linda's persistent efforts, Willy habitually uses a trumped-up version of his past or future as a ready antidote to reality.

Because they float far above the realities of life, family, and work, these fantasies have a perfection that makes them vastly more attractive than messy and disappointing realities. This gives fanciful but unrealistic dreams enormous staying power. The scariest aspect of Willy's situation is that he does, at times, see things for what they are, but he uses his dreams to block these glimpses of reality.

Everyone around Willy knew the story: he wasn't an impressive individual, he wasn't well liked, and his modest success as a salesman was the result of dogged effort, not talent and charm. Willy was never going to be "big." And he should have known this because the evidence was right in front of him: the size of his paychecks, the long hours he put in, his family's struggle to make ends meet, and the fact that he spent years as a road man and never moved up in his company. Willy wasn't a superstar and didn't have the makings of one, which made him cling even harder to his dreams.

What distinguishes a realistic dream from a delusive and potentially destructive fantasy? Willy's experiences suggest two answers. One is that defective dreams need to be pumped up, frequently and vigorously. The Loman family has a near-ritual, led by Willy, in which everyone joins forces to "buck Willy up," regardless of reality. On the day before Willy kills himself, everyone knows how bad things are. Willy is working on straight commission, earning nothing, and living off Charley's loans. Biff has been a drifter for years, spent time in jail for stealing, and is enraged at his father. Everyone knows about the rubber hose in the cellar.

So how does the family spend the evening? By talking feverishly about the preposterous idea that Biff and his brother Happy will form water polo teams and tour around the country promoting a Loman line of sporting goods. The reality is that they have no teams, no financing, no reputation, and no sporting goods, but Willy declares it a "million-dollar idea" and says, "You guys together could absolutely lick the civilized world." The reality facing this family is ominous, so a brief excursion to a castle in the sky might be excusable, but too much of Loman family life involves the inflation of Willy's dreams.

The other sign of delusive dreams is fragility. At times, Willy resorts to harsh tactics to protect his grandiose view of himself and his sons' future. For example, Linda tries several times to say something about the Loman Brothers line of sporting goods. Willy, fearing she will inject a dose of common sense, repeatedly and rudely cuts her off. Linda can't even finish a sentence. This scene in the play is ugly and deeply dismaying: as Willy's house of cards grows higher and higher, he must protect it at all costs.

Like Linda, Willy's brother Ben has a very pragmatic view of what makes a good dream: there is something "one can feel with the hand." Ben is referring to tangible objects such as cash and diamonds, but he follows the same approach Linda did when she heard Willy say he'd sold twelve hundred gross and then calculated what he had earned. Both Linda and Ben can dream, but they don't kid themselves about realities around them. In contrast, Willy's dreams are gossamer—fragile and fanciful.

The best leaders have tested and strengthened their dreams on the anvil of hard fact and actual experience. When Clara Barton, the founder of the American Red Cross, heard that Civil War soldiers were dying for lack of supplies, she organized a relief effort. Then she went further, taking the supplies to the battlefields, where she treated soldiers with split-open heads, crushed limbs, and badly torn flesh. Once, a bullet ripped through her dress and killed the man she was treating. Barton was called "the angel of the battlefield" for her soaring ideals and because she immersed herself, again and again, in the hellish carnage of battle. Clara Barton's image of a good life could stand the test of daylight scrutiny. Willy's dreams are a refuge from the reality of his life and work, not a reflection of it, and therefore a serious danger to himself and those around him.

Which Dreams Will You Abandon?

The standard criticism of Willy is that he had the wrong dream. Biff says this at his father's graveside, and some critics believe Willy pursued a toxic version of the American dream. But this is too simple. Willy had many dreams—too many, in fact—and not just a single bad one. He could not make the hard choices that good dreams require.

Willy wants to be a great salesman. He wants love and respect from everyone around him and from his family. He longs to be an adventurer, like his father and brother. He envies his brother's wealth. Willy dreams his sons will become worldly, rich, and important. He wants to start a business of his own—to get off the road and leave something to his wife and sons. He loves to build things with his hands. Willy dreams of a business world where personal relationships are central, and not prices and deals. And he longs for a simple life, where he can get back to the good times with Biff, which "used to be so full of light, and comradeship, the sleigh-riding in winter, and the ruddiness on his cheeks."

Willy is a human version of the Pushmi-pullyu, an imaginary creature that looks like a llama and has heads pointing in opposite directions. This is very dangerous for Willy, and ultimately for his family. The ceaseless contest among his many dreams leaves him unfocused and confused. A dismaying aspect of his story is that he lives almost all his life with so little clarity about what he really wants. Because he never figures out what he really wants, Willy is vulnerable to pressures outside him and to impulses within.

Willy lives in a tough, confusing, and sometimes cruel world—he is a weak salesman and the sole breadwinner during the harsh Depression years, and Biff is right when he tells Willy that people like the two of them are a dime a dozen. In this intensely competitive world, Willy's jumble of dreams and aspirations leaves him quite vulnerable. When his boss fires him, Willy yells at him and says, "I put thirty-four years into this firm, Howard, and now I can't pay my insurance! You can't eat the orange and throw the peel away—a man is not a piece of fruit!" But Howard does just this, and Willy is completely unprepared for it because of his delusion that he is "vital" to his company in New England.

The worst vulnerabilities created by Willy's dreams are emotional and psychological. His terrible fight with Biff ends abruptly when Biff starts crying, right after telling Willy to burn his phony dreams. Willy says, "Isn't that—isn't that remarkable. Biff—he likes me!" Linda tells him, "He loves you,

Willy." Here, after many long years of silence and pain, is a chance for a father and son to recapture the love they once shared. But another of Willy's dreams crushes this moment. Willy says, "That boy—that boy is going to be magnificent," and he immediately begins imagining what Biff will accomplish with twenty thousand dollars in his pocket—in other words, with the insurance proceeds from Willy's suicide.

Willy's mind and heart are a grab bag of competing hopes and dreams. Some conflict with others: his longing for Biff's love is at odds with his fervent hope that Biff will become wealthy and important. Some dreams blind Willy and keep him from seeing who he is and all he has actually accomplished during the long, hard years of the Great Depression. His family owns a car and is months away from paying off the mortgage. Linda loves him deeply, and is doing all she can to care for him while his life is falling apart. And she loves Willy for who he is: she shares his "turbulent longings" and knows full well that "he's not the finest character who ever lived."

Willy's experience suggests that having too many dreams can be as destructive as a bleak, defeatist way of life. Willy's batch of unexamined hopes and aspirations confused, misled, and subverted him, and the destructive consequences metastasized throughout his family. One of the dreams Willy pursued so tenaciously—his sad hope for celebrity, wealth, and status—brought him little real happiness and wreaked havoc in his family. We usually view leadership as something that takes place in public life, typically in companies or government. But families are the building blocks of society, and the leadership of parents is every bit as vital and challenging as leadership elsewhere. Hence, when parents fail in this responsibility, as Willy did, the results can be profound.

When Biff, standing by his father's grave, says his father didn't know who he was, he reminds us that Willy was never clear about what he really wanted. Dreams resist pragmatism, as they should, and few people sit down and rank-order their life's aspirations. Yet Willy's experience suggests that an important test of a good dream can be the willingness to sacrifice other dreams for it. Willy couldn't do this. Yet even the greatest leaders, with all their extraordinary talents, have had to make great sacrifices to pursue what they valued most. Commitment to a dream for life or work usually has real costs—and, as Linda Loman would put it, "attention must be paid."

Are These Really My Dreams?

Perhaps the saddest aspect of Willy's dreams is that many of them aren't his. They are commodity dreams, grabbed off the shelf of mass culture. And, even more dismaying, the people close to Willy understand this and try to warn him, but he won't listen. For example, Willy dreams of being an all-star salesman and thinks that selling is basically a matter of relationships—success, he believes, depends on being liked or, even better, on being well liked—but Willy isn't very good at relationships, and his real talents lie elsewhere.

At the beginning of the play, Charley compliments Willy on the living room ceiling he has put up. Charley says that this kind of work is a mystery to him and asks how Willy did it. Most people would appreciate the kind words and answer the question, but not Willy. He asks Charley if he's planning to put up a ceiling himself and, when Charley, says no, tells him to stop bothering him about the ceiling. Then he adds that a man who can't handle tools isn't really a man. At Willy's graveside, Charley says that Willy "was a happy man with a batch of cement," and Linda adds that he was wonderful with his hands. Biff says there was more of Willy in the front porch he built than in all the sales he ever made. Everyone seems to know that Willy really loved making things with his hands and was very good at it.

Would Willy's life have been better if he had worked as a carpenter? We can only speculate about this, but Charley's comment—that Willy was a happy man with a batch of concrete—is quite telling. It reminds us that we never see Willy genuinely happy. The closest he comes are his spasms of deluded excitement about Biff. How can we tell the difference between a dream that grows naturally out of a person's needs and experiences and one that is crudely spliced into his or her life? Willy's experiences suggest three practical ways of thinking about this question.

The Love of Drudgery. Charley's graveside comment suggests one way to find a good dream. Working with cement is not most people's idea of fun—it is hard, messy, demanding work. But Willy enjoyed it, and not because it was a cheap way to get a new porch. He simply liked the work.

The British essayist Logan Pearsall Smith wrote, "The test of a vocation is the love of the drudgery it involves." Unfortunately, Willy never applies this unorthodox wisdom to his life. Instead, he pays far too much attention to what he dreams of getting and too little to his lived experience of trying to get it. This is another way in which Willy's dreams float high in the clouds, barely tethered to reality. He wants Ben's wealth, his worldly wisdom, and his rugged assurance; the respect and comradeship Dave Singleman had earned; his father's freedom and pluck; and Charley's prosperous little business. Willy chose a career in sales, but he isn't particularly good at it and there is no evidence he enjoys selling.

The biographies of many successful people show their lifelong delight in activities that others find hard or tedious. Rupert Murdoch, the Australian-American entrepreneur and deal maker, controls a global media empire of satellite networks, cable businesses, and Hollywood studios, but his enduring love is the newspaper pressroom. Murdoch, for example, remained devoted to the profitless *New York Post*. One biographer wrote, "Murdoch was almost besotted with the *Post* . . . A major newspaper office, with the roar and the smell and the grime of the presses and its power in the community, had exhilarated him all his life . . . As Alexander Cockburn put it in the *Wall Street Journal*, for Murdoch to sell the *New York Post* 'would be like Dracula selling his coffin.'"

Willy, in contrast, is obsessed with the destination and takes little delight in the journey. For example, he never mentions what he sells, as if it really doesn't matter. Another symptom of this problem—for Willy and many real-life failures—is a preoccupation with shortcuts. Willy's favorite shortcut—the alternative to patience, training, and hard work—is being well liked. When Biff was basking in the glory of high school football triumphs, Willy thought his son's future was guaranteed. At one point, Charley, another realist, asks bluntly, "Why must everybody like you? Who liked J.P. Morgan? Was he impressive? In a Turkish bath he'd look like a butcher. But with his pockets on he was very well liked." Charley's comment should have been a devastating blow to Willy's faith in quick-and-easy solutions, but Willy doesn't even acknowledge it. If Willy really liked his job, or even just part of it, in the way he liked working with his hands, shortcuts would not have been his private religion.

Dead or Alive? Willy's tragedy suggests a second way of distinguishing healthy and unhealthy dreams. Unhealthy dreams, like Willy's, are static and lifeless. When Willy was young, he dreamt of wealth and of passing prosperity on to his sons. When he is old, broken down, and out of work, he has the same dream. When Willy was young and his sons were children, he dreamed they would some day be great. Two decades later, after Biff has spent years drifting from job to job, Willy wants to believe his son is just around the corner from greatness. Willy says, "Certain men just don't get started till later in life. Like Thomas Edison, I think. Or B.F. Goodrich." There may have even been a gleam in Willy's eye as he left home to crash his car and die, because of the insurance money he thought Biff would get.

Healthy dreams are different. As individuals move through life. they grow, evolve, and reshape themselves. And sometimes, when dreams no longer give life and vitality, they fade away. Everyone around Willy understands this. Linda tells him, "life is a casting off." Charley tells Willy to just forget about Biff, saying harshly, "When a deposit bottle is broken, you don't get your deposit back." And Biff, as we have seen, tells Willy to burn his phony dreams.

But Willy can't take this advice. His dreams are cast in iron. They never evolve, and so they confine and distort his life. Willy can never acknowledge that Biff has grown up, that he can no longer influence or shape his son, that his efforts to do so only drive Biff further away, and that his own career and life are drawing to a close and there are some things he will never achieve.

Really Listening. Until recently, the unconscious mind was viewed, in Freudian terms, as a cauldron of primal instincts. Now, cognitive neuroscience compares it to a computer operating system. In other words, much of our mind operates silently, powerfully, and inaccessibly. Unconscious forces structure and drive much of what we perceive, feel, think, and do. We are often, as the title of a recent study puts it, strangers to ourselves—just as Willy is. Scores of studies confirm what Willy's sad life suggests. We just don't know ourselves as well as we think, and others often know us better. If Willy had been able to listen to the people around him, particularly Linda, he might have built his dreams on the solid foundations of what he really cared about.

Even the best leaders need others' help to understand themselves. James Burke, the highly regarded former head of Johnson & Johnson, once recounted a painful but valuable example. Burke had just been given an important job at the company, at a very early age, when his new boss told him:

> You're a bachelor and you're having a lot of fun in New York. I'll accept that you're bright. I'll accept that you can bring a lot to the business. I'll even accept that maybe Bobby Johnson is right about you, that you can some day run this

company. But I don't see that in you. And I don't see any indication that you want to pay the price to do it. Now, if you do we'll take it a step at a time. You have this job for a year, and this door is open, whenever you want me I'm available.

Burke later said, "He really gave it to me, and he was right." A clear sign of Burke's capacity to grow into a leader is that he could actually hear this comment and respond to it, even though it hurt. In contrast, when Willy hears similar concerns from Linda, he lashes back in anger or retreats to dreams.

My Dream or Our Dream?

Willy's dreams stifle him and his family for another reason, one that is best understood through another classic story. *Of Mice and Men* is John Steinbeck's famous portrait of an extraordinary friendship between two men. One of them, Lennie, is huge, extremely strong, childlike, and mentally handicapped. The other, George, is small, wiry, quick-minded, and generous. George has been taking care of Lennie for several years. Their story ends tragically: Lennie kills a woman—he wants to feel her hair, she resists, and he accidentally breaks her neck—and George then kills Lennie, moments before a lynch mob would have captured him.

George and Lennie's story has several similarities to Willy's. Like Biff, the two men are drifters. The Great Depression looms in the background of both stories. Both involve powerful, captivating dreams, and both stories end with death. But George and Lennie's dream is very different from Willy's. Their minds aren't jumbled like his: they know what they want. Their dream is modest, and they never fantasize about greatness. All they want is to stop drifting and to support themselves, and Lennie wants rabbits to play with. George puts his hopes this way: "S'pose they was a carnival or a circus come to town, or a ball game, or any damn thing . . . We'd just go to her . . . We wouldn't ask nobody if we could. Jus' say, 'We'll go to her,' an' we would. Jus' milk the cow and sling some grain to the chickens an' go to her."

Most important, George and Lennie share their dream. As we have seen, Willy's dreams tyrannize Linda and drive Biff away. In contrast, George and Lennie are drawn closely together by their dream. This is George's beautiful, lyrical description of what their dream means in their lives:

> Guys like us, that work on ranches, are the loneliest guys in the world. They got no family. They don't belong no place ... With us it ain't like that. We got a future. We got somebody to talk to that gives a damn about us. We don't have to sit in no bar room blowin' in our jack jus' because we got no place else to go. If them other guys gets in jail they can rot for all anybody gives a damn. But not us.

Then Lennie says, "But not us! An' why? ... because I got you to look after me, and you got me to look after you, and that's why."

The dream George and Lennie share is an inspiring image, and the contrast with Willy is dramatic. He is truly "a man way out there in the blue." There is, of course, a romantic appeal to lone dreamers and adventurers; sometimes they see and do things no one else can. But Willy's dreams isolate him. For most people, who work in organizations and live in communities and families, his solitary aspirations are a serious warning.

Pragmatic Dreams

An old Irish adage says, "In dreams begin responsibilities." Willy's tragedy shows clearly that good dreams for work and life are not vague musings or lovely white clouds in a soft blue sky. Dreams have real and pervasive consequences, particularly the dreams of men and women with power over others.

Willy, of course, is not the leader of an organization. As a parent, however, he is a leader of a family, with enormous power over the lives of his sons. His dreams dramatically changed their lives, as can the dreams and driving passions of the men and women who lead organizations today. Willy's story suggests that, from time to time, leaders need to look carefully, even critically, at their deepest hopes and aspirations. The hard question for them is whether their dreams are healthy or not—for themselves and for those who depend on their leadership and judgment.

In these reflections, Linda Loman's voice needs to be louder than Willy's. Good dreams have deep roots in a person's character and everyday life, not in the images and seductions of the society around them. They survive T.E. Lawrence's test of daylight scrutiny. Love of drudgery may be a better test of a healthy dream than excitement or inspiration. Good dreams reshape themselves as time goes by, and they deepen and strengthen relationships with other people.

Willy Loman Is Undone by the American Dream

Thomas E. Porter

Thomas E. Porter is a professor of English at the University of Texas at Arlington. He has written several articles on Miller and his works.

Porter draws attention to Arthur Miller's fascination with the 1929 stock market crash and its effects and asserts that the crash's temporary destruction of the proverbial American Dream led to a depression that went far beyond a lack of funds. Willy Loman is under the spell of the same American Dream, which Porter describes as a myth. Despite the support of friends and family, the cutthroat world of sales weighs too heavily on him. Porter recognizes that Willy may have fared better in life had he been a carpenter rather than a salesman. However, the illusion of success defeats Willy in the end as he considers suicide the means to fulfill a social and self-created myth.

The most salient quality of Arthur Miller's tragedy of the common man *Death of a Salesman* is its Americanism. This quality in the play is demonstrated by the contrasting re- actions of American and English reviewers. The English took the hero at face value and found little of interest in his person or his plight:

> There is almost nothing to be said for Loman who lies to himself as to others, has no creed or philosophy of life be- yond that of making money by making buddies, and cannot even be faithful to his helpful and long-suffering wife.

Thomas E. Porter, "Acres of Diamonds: *Death of a Salesman*," *Myth and Modern American Drama*, Detroit: Wayne State University Press, 1969, pp. 144–52. Copyright © 1969 by Wayne State University Press. All rights reserved. Reproduced with permis- sion of the Wayne State University Press and the author.

Brooks Atkinson, on the other hand, thought Willy "a good man who represents the homely, decent, kindly virtues of a middle-class society." The Englishman treats Willy with regard for his American context, the New York reviewer sees him as the representative of a large segment of American society. When the literary critics measure the play against Greek and Elizabethan drama, they agree with the English evaluation; the hero seems inadequate. His lack of stature, his narrow view of reality, his obvious character defects diminish the scope of the action and the possibilities of universal application. Against a large historical perspective and without the American context, the salesman is a "small man" who fails to cope with his environment. But for better or worse, Miller's hero is not simply an individual who has determined on an objective and who strives desperately to attain it; he is also representative of an American type, the Salesman, who has accepted an ideal shaped for him and pressed on him by forces in his culture. This ideal is the matrix from which Willy emerges and by which his destiny is determined. It is peculiarly American in origin and development—seed, flower and fruit. For Arthur Miller's salesman is a personification of the success myth; he is committed to its objectives and defined by its characteristics. *Salesman* deals with the [nineteenth-century American writer] Horatio Alger ideal, the rags-to-riches romance of the American dream. . . .

The "success" structure in the play, as the critic immediately recognizes, is not the whole *Salesman* story. As the English critic sees Willy as a detestable little man, the American sees him as a pathetic figure who suffers deeply. The pathetic quality is produced by the playwright's emphasis on the culture that shaped the salesman's personality. The pressures of economic growth in urban society created the salesman mystique and these same forces punish the unsuccessful inexorably. The 1929 [stock market] crash impressed Miller greatly:

> The hidden laws of fate lurked not only in the characters of people, but equally if not more imperiously in the world beyond the family parlor. Out there were the big gods, the ones whose disfavor could turn a proud and prosperous and dignified man into a frightened shell of a man whatever he thought of himself, and whatever he decided or didn't decide to do.

These powers were economic crisis and political imperatives at whose mercy man found himself. The myth holds them at bay, overcomes them, puts the successful man out of their reach. As antihero, the salesman (and his family) is at their mercy. Time-installment buying, the enclosure of the house by apartments, the impersonal attitude of the executive illustrate these external forces. If these "hidden gods" decide to doom a generation, they can grind exceeding small. When the stock market crashed, once safe and happy millionaires left by the window. The common man does not control such a phenomenon, and the success myth does not take such catastrophes into account. Willy's faith in the myth leaves him vulnerable to the big gods. No version of the success myth really equips anyone to deal with these forces.

Neighbors and the Family Unit

One solution to coping with this impersonal culture is a concomitant impersonality in dealing with it. Miller dramatizes this reaction in his depiction of the good neighbors, Charley and Bernard. Charley is a successful businessman in a minor way; Bernard, the bespectacled tag-along, is a successful lawyer. Out of the goodness of his heart, Charles supports Willy and Linda by "loaning" the salesman fifty dollars a week. He drops by to play cards with Willy and generally tolerates his blustering irritability. He offers Willy a steady job. He is the lone unrelated mourner at the funeral. Out of the salesman's own mouth, the bitter truth is that Charley is the only friend he has. The good neighbor has no theory about success, no magic formula but unconcern: "My salvation is that I never took any interest in anything." He never preached at his son or exhibited any interest in success or money. Without preaching, Charley goes about doing good. It is not clear where all the virtue this good neighbor displays springs from. He is the good Samaritan for whose conduct no explanation need be given. More significantly, though Charley makes no concessions to the cult of success in his actions or his manner, he knows the rules: "The only thing you got in this world is what you can sell."

Bernard is the opposite number to Biff and Happy. He, too, is a good neighbor. Though his boyhood relations with the Lomans kept him a subordinate, he holds no grudge, is still sincerely interested in Biff and respectful with Willy. Bernard has followed his father's example, if not his counsel.

Bernard. Goodby, Willy, and don't worry about it. You know, "If at first you don't succeed . . ."

Willy. Yes, I believe in that.

Bernard. But sometimes, Willy, it's better for a man just to walk away.

The successful lawyer has no other word for Willy, except perhaps a footnote to the success formula; he points out that Biff never prepared himself for anything. Charley and Bernard really have no alternate faith to offer Willy. They show a distrust of the big gods and treat them gingerly. Otherwise, they are good people who sympathize with the Lomans' plight, who understand their aspirations without emulating them, who put friendship above the law. They bear witness to the vacuity of success worship, but provide no faith with which to replace it.

This is not to say that Miller suggests no alternative. On the one hand, he suggests a family solidarity centering around the wife and mother; on the other, he tentatively offers a retreat from the competitive business world to an agrarian, manual-labor society. Linda is the heart of the family. She is wise, warm, sympathetic. She knows her husband's faults and her sons' characters. For all her frank appraisals, she loves them. She is contrasted with the promiscuous sex symbolized by the Woman and the prostitutes. They operate in the world outside as part of the impersonal forces that corrupt. Happy equates his promiscuity with taking manufacturers' bribes, and Willy's Boston woman can "put him right through to the buyers." Linda holds the family together—she keeps the accounts, encourages her husband, tries to protect him from heartbreak. She becomes the personification of Family, that social unity in which the individual has a real identity.

The concepts of Father and Mother and so on were received by us unawares before the time we were conscious of ourselves as selves. In contrast, the concepts of Friend, Teacher, Employee, Boss, Colleague, Supervisor, and the many other social relations come to us long after we have gained consciousness of ourselves, and are therefore outside ourselves. They are thus in an objective rather than a subjective category. In any case what we feel is always more "real" to us than what we know, and we feel the family relationship while we only know the social one.

"Silence and Support" of Wife and Mother

If Willy is not totally unsympathetic (and he is not), much of the goodness in him is demonstrated in his devotion to his wife, according to his lights. Though he is often masterful and curt, he is still deeply concerned about her: "I was fired, and I'm looking for a little good news to tell your mother, because the woman has waited and the woman has suffered." While planting his garden, in conversation with Ben, he mutters: "'Cause she's suffered, Ben, the woman has suffered." Biff is attached to his mother, and Happy's hopelessness is most graphic in his failure to be honest with, or concerned about, his family. The family's devotion to one another, even though misguided, represents a recognizable American ideal.

Linda, for all her warmth and goodness, goes along with her husband and sons in the best success-manual tradition. She tries to protect them from the forces outside and fails. The memory of her suffering and her fidelity does not keep Willy and Happy from sex or Biff from wandering. Miller's irony goes still deeper. While Linda is a mirror of goodness and the source of the family's sense of identity, she is no protection—by her silence and her support, she unwittingly cooperates with the destructive myth. Linda follows the rules laid down by the self-help advocates. She is a good home manager, she understands and encourages her husband, she keeps her house neat and is a good mother. [Entrepreneur and educator Roger W.] Babson recommends a good wife as a major factor in working toward success: "A good wife and well-kept house and some healthy children are of the utmost importance in enabling one to develop the six 'I's' of success and to live the normal, wholesome, upright life." Linda stays in her place, never questioning out loud her husband's objectives and doing her part to help him achieve them.

The Lomans Belonged in a Different Era

As another possible alternative to the success myth, Miller proposes a return to a non-competitive occupation in an agrarian or trade-oriented society. In the context of *Death of a Salesman* he makes this offer, not explicitly as a universal panacea, but in terms of the Lomans' problem. The good days of hope and promise in the play are connected with a warm sun and clusters of trees in the neighborhood, fresh air and gardening. The reminiscence sequences are marked by this scenic change: "The apartment houses are fading out and the entire house and surroundings become covered with leaves." The neighborhood once bloomed with lilac, wisteria, peonies and daffodils, but now it is "bricks and windows, windows and bricks," and over-population. Willy is a talented work-man; he has practically rebuilt the house: "All the cement, the lumber, the reconstruction I put in this house! There ain't a crack to be found in it any more." Biff, who understands this strength in his father, has actually escaped to the West. His ambition to succeed conflicts with the satisfaction he finds on the farm:

> This farm I work on, it's spring there now, see? And they've got about fifteen new colts. There's nothing more inspiring or—beautiful than the sight of a mare and a new colt. And it's cool there now, see? Texas is cool now and it's spring.

Biff suspects that perhaps the Lomans have been miscast in their salesman role:

> They've laughed at Dad for years, and you know why? Be-cause we don't belong in this nuthouse of a city! We should be mixing cement on some open plain, or—or carpenters. A carpenter is allowed to whistle!

So when Biff comes to realize who he is, his insight flashes out of the contrast between the office and the open sky. The things he loves in the world are "the work and the food and time to sit and smoke." And his obituary for his father is a memorial to the good days when Willy was working on the house: "There's more of him in that front stoop than in all the sales he ever made." Charley agrees that Willy was "a happy man with a bunch of cement." In a freer, older society, the doomed salesman might have been a happy man.

The pathos of this situation—the square peg in a round hole—is dramatized in the garden scene. After the ordeal in the office and the restaurant, Willy feels the impulse to plant as an imperative: "I've got to get some seeds, right away.... I don't have a thing in the ground." He then begins to plant his garden in the barren patch beside the house by flashlight. All the contradictions in the salesman's life come into focus. His instinct to plant, to put something that will grow in the ground, is ineffectual—he must work by artificial light, surrounded by apartment houses, in the hard-packed dirt. The seeds will not grow; Willy, who was going to mine diamonds in Brooklyn, reverts to hoeing and planting, but the urbanization of his world has already defeated him. As he plants, he talks "business" with Ben. His suicide will bring twenty thousand "on the barrelhead." This insurance money is the diamond he sees shining in the dark. All the forces that conspired to make—and break—Willy Loman are gathered here. His instinct to produce from the earth, the happy farmer he might have been, is frustrated by the society that has boxed him in. The dream of diamonds and his idealization of Ben have "rung up a zero"; the only way he can make his life pay off is by self-destruction.

Willy Personifies the American Myth

Taken at the level of parable, the play presents the failure of the success myth by destroying the Horatio Alger image of the rags-to-riches triumph of the common man. This view of the play considers Willy as Salesman, Linda as Family, Ben as Success, and the moral of the play is the fall of the Golden Calf. But Miller has not written a morality play in *Salesman*, nor does he make the mistake of preaching. The audience says, "That's the way middle-class America lives and thinks"; it also says: "I know a man just like that." The Willy Lomans who see the play do not recognize themselves and respond to Willy's collapse with the now legendary remark: "That New England territory was no damned good!" Wrapped in the trappings of instruction is the deep personal anguish of a contemporary American that audiences can recognize.

Willy the Salesman represents all those Americans caught in the mesh of the myth and the moral pressures it generates. As a type, he is a product of social and economic forces outside himself. But in his struggle with those forces, Willy is also a suffering human being. He battles to retain his faith, is shaken by doubts about his ability to live according to his belief, humiliates himself to discover the secret that lies at its heart. His blind commitment to his ideal is wholehearted, and if Willy the Salesman is necessarily destroyed by that commitment, the audience feels that Willy the person is worth saving.

Thus, when he goes to his death without knowing why he has lived or why he is dying, he fulfills the destiny of the type, but as an individual who has suffered, he remains unfulfilled. The Salesman can neither suffer nor be converted (he would then cease to be Salesman), but the family man—the husband and father and friend—does suffer and, by virtue of it, can change. If Willy were only abstract set of stereotyped characteristics, a figure in a morality play, there would be little sympathy for his plight. In the "Requiem" epilogue, the various aspects of Willy's character come in for comment. Biff's epitaph considers what Willy might have been, the happy carpenter, the outdoorsman. Charley, on the other hand, reads the apologia for the Salesman:

> Nobody dast blame this man. You don't understand: Willy was a salesman. And for the salesman, there is no rock bottom to life. He don't put a bolt to a nut, he don't tell you the law or give you medicine. He's a man way out there in the blue, riding on a smile and a shoeshine. And when they start not smiling back—that's an earthquake. And then you get yourself a couple of spots on your hat, and you're finished. Nobody dast blame this man. A salesman is got to dream, boy. It comes with the territory.

This speech defends Willy in the context of myth and moral, but as a justification of his uncomprehending self-destruction, it fails to consider the individual who suffered through his life and rang up a zero at the end. Linda, the long-suffering, says the last word for the husband and the father:

> Willy, dear, I can't cry. Why did you do it? I search and I search and I search, and I can't understand it, Willy. I made

the last payment on the house today. Today, dear. And there'll be nobody home. . . . We're free and clear. . . . We're free.

Linda cannot understand the mystery as Willy could not understand it. Suffering and sacrifice, for the family, have led to the "freedom" of an empty house and the grave.

Illusion Defeats the Salesman

Miller, who set out to write the tragedy of the common man, is finally trapped both by the myth he is denouncing and by the dramatic form he has chosen. The salesman's version of the success myth—the cult of personality—is shown to be a tissue of false values that lead only to frustration. Miller dramatizes the problem of guilt and the reality of Willy's suffering because of his values, but, try as he may, he can neither bring Willy to an insight by which he understands his failure nor find a societal strategy that can absolve him of it. The traditional tragic pattern of action demands an epiphany, a purgation and a renewal that does not cancel the suffering of the protagonist, but that does make sense of it. Miller recognizes this demand of the form and struggles to fulfill it; in the end the myth defeats him.

At the level of dianoia, the conscious treatment of values, Miller tries to find a replacement for the success myth and fails:

> This confusion [about "true" and "false" values] is abetted by the greater clarity of the rejected values which are embodied in the dream of success. The false dream is fully and vividly sketched; positive values seem rather dim and conventional.

The false values, tightly woven into Willy's personality, are clearly destructive. But when Biff, the man who "knows who he is," advocates a return to the farm, it becomes clear how meager are the resources of the culture for coping with Willy's problem. The return to a pre-Alger agrarian way of life is an example of nostalgia for the garden; turning back the clock is no solution for a million city-dwelling Willy Lomans who left the farm to seek their fortunes. Charley's detachment from the myth does not supply a positive answer either. For Charley, whether he cares about it or not, *is* a success; he owns his small business and supports Willy. If the successful must protect the failures, then Willy's values are not altogether false, and the common man who cannot get along with the myth cannot get along without it either.

Society cannot absolve Willy; it can only understand and sympathize. Understanding and sympathy are not enough; Willy still goes to his "freedom" in the grave uncomprehending. At the level of dramatic action, there is no epiphany in which suffering leads to insight, that moment of revelation when the hero sees himself and his situation clearly, understands what he has lost, and finds the path to regeneration. Willy has suffered, but, because he is the Salesman, his suffering does not bring him to understanding. Miller recognizes this difficulty also and tries to circumvent it by promoting Biff to hero, by giving him the insight of which Willy was incapable. Nonetheless, it is Willy's fate that concerns us. He must go to his death hapless and deluded, but his end leaves the play without that final stage which the conventional tragic structure demands. Like the defective-hero, the Salesman cannot acknowledge his mistake without also destroying his identity.

In *Death of a Salesman* Miller taps a popular formula for the structure of his drama. Although the Dale Carnegie approach, the cult of personality, is on the wane in the present generation, the drive for success is very much alive. Willy's plight, grounded in the excesses of a previous generation but fostered by attitudes still shared by the present generation, draws from the audience both recognition of the illusion and sympathy for the visionary. Willy's suffering is real and deep. America cannot accept the success myth—"Horatio Alger" is now a term of derision—but there is no real substitute for it. Because Miller has built his play around an American dream, he strikes deep into the consciousness of the audience. The contemporary American, because he cannot solve the dilemma either, becomes involved in the sufferings of Willy the person as he watches the death of Willy the Salesman.

Alienation from His Work Drives Willy Loman to Suicide

Paul Blumberg

Paul Blumberg is professor emeritus of sociology at Queens College, City University of New York.

In the following selection, Blumberg examines Arthur Miller's plays from a sociological perspective, asserting that Willy Loman represents the typical alienated white-collar worker of the mid-twentieth-century corporate world. Blumberg states that Willy's unhappiness results from internalizing others' goals and from his failure to live up to their expectations.

If, as sociologist, one wanted to play the devil's advocate for a moment, one might argue that of the two forms of the study of social man in contemporary society, sociology on the one hand, and the social novel or the social play on the other hand, it is truly the social novel or play which offers the more incisive social analysis.

The sociologist, the argument would go, merely provides us at most with a series of generalizations which represents the culmination of research involving concepts, hypotheses, empirical regularities and so on. By providing the generalizations at various levels of abstraction, or perhaps in linking these together in some more or less systematic fashion, the sociologist regards his task as essentially *completed*.

But the social novelist or the social playwright, on the other hand, cannot be content to stop at the level of generalization; indeed, he must make the sociological generalization *his point of departure*. At the level of generalization, the social novelist or playwright is just beginning, because he must now

Paul Blumberg, "Sociology and Social Literature: Work Alienation in the Plays of Aurthur Miller," *American Quarterly*, vol. 21, no. 2, summer 1969, pp. 291–310. Copyright © 1969 The Johns Hopkins University Press. Reproduced by permission.

take that generalization and proceed to illustrate it, to drama-
tize it, to particularize it imaginatively in the form of a scene,
an act, an episode, a chapter, a story or an entire novel or
play. The generalization which for the sociologist is a finished
product is for the fiction writer, with sociological inclinations,
merely the barest raw material. In this sense—without forget-
ting the dissimilarity of their tasks, purposes, objectives or
methods—the social novelist or dramatist is truly the sociologist par excellence, because he must carry the sociological generalization to a further and more sophisticated point.

Literature as Social Documentation

Whether one would agree with the perhaps overstated argument sketched above, it is nonetheless becoming increasingly
recognized that, in spite of the pseudo-scientific and rather
philistine objections of some of the more enthusiastic positiv-
ists in sociology, social novels and drama have a definite place
in illustrating and exploring sociological principles with a
force, realism and emotional content which sociological essays
are by their very nature incapable of doing. Literature is a rich
form of social documentation, illuminating the norms and
values and entire culture of our own and previous eras, and
the sociologist who ignores literature is thereby neglecting an
invaluable source of sociological insight. In this regard [soci-
ologist] Lewis Coser has pointed to an important paradox,
that while sociologists often rely on the casual, untrained
community informant as a source of data, they ignore the
trained and keen observations of the imaginative writer.

What I have endeavored to do in this essay, then, is to
demonstrate how imaginative literature—in this case, the dramatic form—can be used to illustrate and deepen our understanding of ideas commonly employed in sociology. Specifically, I have selected the concept of the "alienation of labor,"
an idea which has been with us in its really modern form
since the days of [nineteenth-century philosopher, political

economist, and revolutionary] Karl Marx, and which in recent years has become of great interest to sociologists and other social commentators. I have attempted to show how one of our greatest contemporary playwrights has incorporated this concept into his work and how an understanding of this theme in Miller's plays can broaden our own perspective of the concept of work alienation. Let us begin, then, with a brief description of how Miller's own background and orientation provide the setting for his dramatic treatment of the alienation of labor.

Playwright as Sociologist

Of all our modern playwrights, Arthur Miller is certainly the one who has the most to say to contemporary sociologists. He is an avid, militant, eager and articulate defender of the "social play." He has written long and often in its defense, declaring that, contrary to critical opinion, the social play need not be synonymous with social *criticism*, although the two are often seen as identical. To summarize Miller's views, a social play, in contrast to a nonsocial or a psychological play, demonstrates the impact of social forces—the class structure, the economy, the system of norms and values, family patterns, etc.—on the raw psychology and lives of the characters; exposes the basic similarity of men, not their uniqueness; and, finally, addresses itself to the question, as did classical Greek drama, which Miller regards as the forerunner of all social plays, "how are we to live?" in a social and humanistic sense.

Miller expressed his basic attitude toward the role of social forces in drama in an address he delivered some years ago in which he said:

> I hope I have made one thing clear . . .—and it is that society is inside of man and man is inside society, and you cannot even create a truthfully drawn psychological entity on the stage until you understand his social relations and their

power to make him what he is and to prevent him from being what he is not. The fish is in the water and the water is in the fish.

Moreover, Miller has constantly reiterated his belief in the futility of a playwright's attempting to explore the psychological side of man in vacuo [in a vacuum], without recourse to his social milieu. Thus, he has written: "I can no longer take with ultimate seriousness a drama of individual psychology written for its own sake, however full it may be of insight and precise observation.". . .

"The Individual" and "the Machine"

The theme of work alienation, the central subject of this essay, is actually a sub-theme in Miller's overall treatment of the alienation of contemporary man from a sense of community or relatedness to others. Although his plays, in themselves, illustrate well the concept of work alienation, he has spelled it out for us, in general terms, in an essay. This will be our point of departure for an examination of some of Miller's plays in which this theme is most apparent. Miller writes:

> The deep moral uneasiness among us, the vast sense of being only tenuously joined to the rest of our fellows, is caused, in my view, by the fact that the person has value as he fits into the pattern of efficiency, and for that alone. The reason *Death of a Salesman*, for instance, left such a strong impression was that it set forth unremittingly the picture of a man who was not even especially "good" but whose situation made clear that at bottom we are alone, valueless, without even the elements of a human person, when once we fail to fit the patterns of efficiency. . . . In short, the absolute value of the individual human being is believed in only as a secondary value; it stands well below the needs of efficient production. We have finally come to serve the machine. The machine must not be stopped, marred, left dirty, or outmoded. Only men can be left marred, stopped, dirty, and alone.

The 1985 television version of Death of a Salesman *starred John Malkovich (left) as Biff and Dustin Hoffman as Willy.* AP Images.

Nor may the exponents of socialism take heart from this. There is no such thing as a capitalist assembly line or dry-goods counter. The disciplines required by machines are the same everywhere and will not be truly mitigated by old-age pensions and social security payments. So long as modern man conceives of himself as valuable only because he fits into some niche in the machine-tending pattern, he will never know anything more than a pathetic doom. . . .

Willy Loman as Alienated White-Collar Worker

Before [sociologist] William Whyte wrote of the organization man and the social ethic, before [sociologist] David Riesman had sketched the characteristics of the modern other-directed man, before [sociologist] C. Wright Mills had given us a bitingly critical portrait of the contemporary personality market in the white collar world, and before [social psychologist]

Erich Fromm's concern of the marketing personality as a characterological type had gained currency—before all of these, Arthur Miller gave us his powerful—nay, definitive—portrait of the prototype of the alienated white collar man in the character of Willy Loman.

In Willy Loman, Marx's concept of work alienation is extended. For Marx, the modern wage worker's labor was alienated in the sense that his work was repetitive, routine, fragmented and dull, that the worker was merely "an appendage to the machine"; that work was for someone else and under someone else's jurisdiction, not one's own; that in his work the worker was separated or alienated from ownership of the factory, the tools with which he works, the product of his labor and so on. But at least the modern wage worker retained spiritual autonomy from the system, retained the means of hating it and withholding commitment to it. But in Willy Loman, as prototype of the alienated white collar worker, both body and soul are thrown into the industrial cauldron, and both are consumed. Willy, a poor victim of a single-minded allegiance to false and hollow values of material success, allows what is most uniquely his, his personality, to be molded, transformed and vulgarized in accordance with what he believes others expect of him. Worse yet, the self-hatred eating at his soul because of his failure to achieve these goals leads him to destroy his precious and once warm relationship with his sons, and finally leads to his own self-destruction. Long before Willy's physical suicide, his self-hatred has brought him to spiritual suicide, and he is only temporarily sustained in his growing madness by his transparent self-deception and dreams of successes past and false illusions of successes future. Willy Loman is, in short, the tragic personification of the other-directed, success-seeking, new middle-class man of mid-20th century corporate America. The incredible impact of this play on American audiences, its reception and acclaim are apt testimony to the fact that Miller captured the emerging social character of the American new middle class.

The Contrast Between "New" Willy and "Old" Ben

In a sociological framework, we see that Miller made a fundamental distinction between the social character of the *old* entrepreneurial middle class and the social character of the *new*, salaried middle class. The contrast between Willy Loman and brother Ben is crucial. In sociological terms, Ben is a classic representative of the old, 19th century middle class, while Willy represents the new, dependent, salaried, pathetically other-directed middle class. Ben's character is clearly inner-directed; he has all the 19th century middle-class virtues: he is hard, unscrupulous, firm, self-reliant, full of the self-confident energy of the 19th century captain of industry or robber baron. While Willy stresses the importance of personality, of being "well liked" and acceptable to the world, of pleasing others, while insisting on proper form, dress, manner and style, Ben ignores all of this. Ben is presented as a satiric caricature of the old, independent entrepreneur. Setting out to make his fortune in Alaska, he instead found himself in Africa because of his "poor sense of direction." But, never mind. Africa: gold, diamonds, riches of all kinds! And he walked into the jungle at seventeen, walked out at twenty-one, and, by God, he was rich! Willy pleads for "the answer," begs Ben for the "secret to success," hanging on his every word. But, just as in the popular American success literature of our day, we get nothing but vague generalities, imprecise slogans and stirring calls to action. Ben's entrepreneurial advice, "Never fight fair with a stranger, boy," sets the competitive old middle-class mood, but it leaves Willy as baffled and helpless as ever.

Compared to Ben, Willy represents another age, another stage in the development of the American economic system. Ben's world is one in which there are still frontiers to cross, new empires to build, before every corner of the economy was organized and incorporated and covered. As an independent agent, self-employed and self-reliant, Ben has no need to rely on the other-directed values of sociability. The key to success for the old middle-class entrepreneur was less his smile than his fist. His independence meant, in essence, that he didn't have to please anyone or be particularly "well liked." As Willy's [neighbor], Charley, says to him at one point after another one of Willy's sermons on popularity-as-a-means-to-salvation: "Why must everybody like you? Who liked J. P. Morgan? Was he impressive?"

Willy's world is different, however. For the new middle-class salaried employee, especially the salesman, success and promotion up the organizational hierarchy *does* depend upon pleasing others: pleasing one's superiors, one's peers, one's customers, one's buyers and a whole host of others. In this respect, Willy was correct: in the world of the salaried new middle class, it is important, crucial, in fact, to be well liked, to sell your personality as well as your "labor power."

As Willy says to Ben, during one of his recurring hallucinations:

> Without a penny to his [Biff's] name, three great universities are begging for him, and from there the sky's the limit, because it's not what you do, Ben. It's who you know and the smile on your face! It's contacts, Ben, contacts! The whole wealth of Alaska passes over the lunch table at the Commodore Hotel, and that's the wonder, the wonder of this country, that a man can end with diamonds here on the basis of being well liked!

And yet, Willy is unsure of his own values, for he seems wedged in transition somewhere between the ideology of an old-fashioned and a contemporary business world. And it is a measure of Willy's insecurity that in this speech he is asking Ben as well as telling him. But this is not Ben's way. He ignores Willy's remarks and only sounds the call to action once more: "There's a new continent at your doorstep, William. You could walk out rich." . . .

Family Relations and Social Relations Clash

One of the persistently recurring themes in Miller's plays is the struggle to realize primary group or *Gemeinschaft* values in a world increasingly dominated by the impersonality of secondary or *Gesellschaft* values, with the ensuing isolation and privatization of life, and the alienation of the individual from his fellows. This clash between "family relations" and "social relations," as Miller calls them, probably finds its most powerful dramatic illustration in *Salesman* when Willy confronts his young boss, Howard.

Willy, sixty-three years of age, is exhausted by his decades of service to the company. He is gradually going mad because of this exhaustion and his self-evident failure to realize the values of material success which he holds so dear, made infinitely worse by the knowledge that his sons, upon whom he has transferred his desperate quest for success, are also both "failures." Willy goes to Howard now to say that he is too ill to travel any more, that Howard must find a place for him in the office. The conversation between Willy and Howard represents the struggle of *Gemeinshaft* with *Gesellshaft* values and the ultimate triumph of the latter. This is not party-line writing, as a few critics once asserted. Howard is not portrayed as the greedy, selfish, heartless capitalist, but merely an understandable victim of the ideology of "business is business," an ideology which has clearly estranged him from any deeper human values. Howard bears Willy no malice, but simply has no place for him in the office; it's simply a matter of dollars and cents: "Kid, I can't take blood from a stone." Not only doesn't Howard have a job for Willy in the office, but, later in the scene, is forced to tell Willy that he has been reluctantly putting off telling him that he can no longer represent the firm at all.

Willy's appeal—so strange and incongruous for a hard-headed salesman—is an appeal to "family relations," to "particularism" in the framework of sociologist Talcott Parsons.

WILLY: God knows, Howard, I never asked a favor of any man. But I was with the firm when your father used to carry you in here in his arms.

Howard: I know that, Willy, but—

WILLY: Your father came to me the day you were born and asked me what I thought of the name of Howard, may he rest in peace.

But all of this is simply irrelevant now. Howard is a stranger and Willy is alone, and the only pertinent point is that Willy is unable to sell any more. Later, as the argument heightens:

Willy: I'm talking about your father! There were promises made across this desk! You mustn't tell me you've got people to see—I put thirty-four years into this firm, Howard, and now I can't pay my insurance! You can't eat the orange and throw the peel away—a man is not a piece of fruit!

And so Willy hammers away helplessly at the invincible doctrine of economic efficiency.

Later, Willy tells Charley that he's been fired: "That snot-nose. Imagine that? I named him. I named him Howard." But Charley only chides him for his naiveté:

Willy, when're you gonna realize that them things don't mean anything? You named him Howard, but you can't sell that. The only thing you got in this world is what you can sell. And the funny thing is that you're a salesman, and you don't know that.

Willy Is a Craftsman in a Business Suit

Willy wasn't really cut out for selling; he was far more talented and gained much more satisfaction working with his hands. As Biff said at the funeral, the memorable days were on Sundays, seeing his father "making the stoop; finishing the cellar; putting on the new porch; when he built the extra bathroom; and put up the garage." Biff adds: "You know something, Charley, there's more of him in that front stoop than in all the sales he ever made." But as happy as he was with this as an avocation, Willy could never have accepted the life of a worker for, as Biff said, "He had all the wrong dreams. All, all wrong." Willy swallowed whole the success ideology of the new middle class; and it eventually poisoned and killed him. Biff, Willy's favorite son, on the other hand, knew the white collar world for what it was—and despised it. He hated the routine of getting on the subway on hot summer mornings, of devoting his whole life to "keeping stock, or making phone calls, or selling or buying. To suffer fifty weeks of the year for the sake of a two-week vacation, when all you really desire is to be outdoors, with your shirt off. And always to have to get ahead of the next fella."

Biff decided to quit this life in spite of his father's desperate urgings, and he went West, into the outdoors, to work on farms, ranches, away from the city, away from a regimented white collar existence. But being Willy's son, he could never quite emancipate himself from the nagging thought that, however free he was in the outdoors, he wasn't getting anywhere; he wasn't "building a future." Willy's suicide finally frees Biff of the last longings he ever had for a middle-class career; he sees finally and powerfully what it did to his father. And, as the play closes, he has firmly decided to go West again, and stay there, and he urges his brother to join him.

But his brother, Happy, draws another lesson from his father's tragedy. He is resolved to succeed where his father has failed, to accept his father's values of material success in an urban, industrial, new middle-class milieu. Where Biff seeks to escape the corroding sense of work alienation that destroyed his father, Happy resolves to win the same game his father has lost. He says resolutely to Biff at his father's grave: "I'm gonna show you and everybody else that Willy Loman did not die in vain. He had a good dream. It's the only dream you can have—to come out number-one man. He fought it out here, and this is where I'm gonna win it for him."

Miller Uses Objects to Convey Failure and Other Themes

Marianne Boruch

Marianne Boruch is an American poet. She developed the Master of Fine Arts program in creative writing at Purdue University, where she has taught since 1987.

In the following essay, Boruch explores the importance of material things in Arthur Miller's plays, examining the ways in which he melds his characters with objects and gestures, creating a larger picture of their humanity. Boruch explains the ways in which Miller used lighting, music, and objects on the stage to broaden the understanding of his characters and enrich his plays' themes. Objects in Death of a Salesman *are personified as characters, often symbolizing the issues that trouble Willy Loman and his family.*

We are faced with a crowd of things: a cracked cylinder head from an old P-40 [fighter plane], a copper pot, silk stockings pressed and gleaming in their cardboard box. We spot a harp, its baseboard somewhat warped yet still quite impressive, golden against a monstrous bureau, or over there, a pile of auto parts: crankshafts, engine pins, grimy axles. Perhaps in the distant left, that's a real tower, dark and frightening, the barbed wire fringe from a past—or future—time. An old radio sits in the dust, and near it, a newspaper curled tightly and torn—in anger?—then dropped. Here's a simple chair, there, a fencer's foil and mask, a football, a fountain pen. We walk around these things, among them; they make an American ruin, a junkyard of moments and desires, fascinating in themselves, but absurd. How does one pull these things into a human focus? The job seems enormous, impossible.

Yet think of the wheelwright, the shipwright. The playwright, is he really any different? Does not this joiner take human and inanimate substance and "work" them together toward some larger end? It was Willy Loman who stated with sudden coherence that, "if a man can't handle tools he's not a man." In speaking of drama, one could widen the remark and venture that a playwright is not a good playwright unless he can take the hard, physical extension of our ideas—things, objects—and use them dramatically, as pivots of human action and revelation. But more than that, one could say a playwright is not a great playwright unless he can use things—in themselves—thematically, not simply as properties to be touched then discarded on the way to discovery, but somehow as the discovery itself. At this point, drama extends itself into poetry, and metaphor swells with movement to a broader, historical reality. Arthur Miller operates in this vision with reserve and intelligence and surprise.

Things Hold Ominous Meaning

He operates such power initially. The touch of any world begins, of course, with what we first see; and in Miller's opening stage demands, we not only find the physical setting depicting time and place, we often are presented with objects that instruct us intuitively through their metaphoric quality. In *All My Sons*, for instance, Miller stages the house and backyard to a kind of Norman Rockwellian perfection, yet the vital element in the setting is the yard's single apple tree, left broken and lifeless by the savage force of the previous night's storm. All opening conversation moves in one way or another around this freak event, and we learn quickly that the tree is more than just a tree. It represents—quite consciously to the characters—the life of the young man, Larry, reported to be missing-in-action, whom some mourn and whom others hope still lives. We realize the intensity of the latter belief because a tree is a hopeful memorial, alive and fruitful; and that a mother should run out into the dark, wet middle of the night to stand in a mute despair at its destruction—as she is reported to have done—immediately presses into icon a rich tension of feeling which is almost effortlessly dramatic. It might be a weak, frivolous idea to structure all action around a missing character, but Miller has solved any possible problem by offering a hard symbolic replacement, thus making such absence seem in fact more powerful than the living presence could probably be. But the tree reveals more. Somewhere in our image-recording subconscious an important seed has been planted. Amid the house and yard and the successful, happy Kellers, seemingly launched full sail into the American dream, something is wrenched and terribly wrong. The only living thing on the place has been broken, suddenly and in darkness split by a broad and violent fact. And we grasp in some strange, inarticulate way that the action will move mysteriously toward revelation of this buried vitality.

Sometimes there is little such mystery about Miller's opening images. As we enter *Death of a Salesman*, witnessing the pressure of those "towering angular shapes" of apartments upon Willy's "fragile-seeming house," the situation seems clear. Hope is losing, and all of the battle will be a sad, desperate business. The apartments appear cool and rational—"a solid vault"—with the self-possession and heartless intention of human manipulators. Through his deliberate staging, drawing the outside world cold and cruel against the inside home "with an air of a dream," Miller has set Willy's point of view indelibly on the reality we are entering. Things brood here, and they break, yet there is possible goodness in that house. As the light takes over the stage, the apartment sky glows its "angry orange" while the Loman house and the forestage are bathed in the frank, simple "blue light of the sky." The two realities exist so far from each other, they have assumed different weather. In this contrast, we instantly feel the weight on Willy's life and realizations; and by the power of the stage images, his helpless exhaustion that opens the play strikes us as more than believable; it seems inevitable.

A similar view operates in the short play *A Memory of Two Mondays*, as Miller works toward an atmosphere partly physically real, partly felt. Yet here the division becomes harder to express imagistically because things move within the location completely; no large, clear comparisons like "outside" and "inside" can be ascertained. Yet the warehouse loft is "surrounded" on all sides by enormous floor-to-ceiling windows, windows ordinarily for light and real world air and color. But these are shut and so encrusted with years of dust that they allow nothing to enter or escape. Everything endures in a strange mix of possibility and oppressive fact. If Miller, in *Death of a Salesman*, had originally wanted the set to be built, literally, in the shape of a skull, the shape of Willy thinking and dreaming back, we have in this set a semi-realization of that wish, a skull-like enclosure, sealed, and thus free-floating in time—indeed, like memory itself. . . .

Miller's Use of "Gesture, Object, and Language"

In *Death of a Salesman*, act one ends in a kind of double exposure as Miller stages two scenes quietly in tandem. A conversation occurs between Willy and Linda upstairs while Biff wanders around in the nighttime kitchen. A rather stunning visual effect takes place, with Miller playing the verbal against its opposite. The pensive Biff comes downstage, the glow of his smoking cigarette circling him in the darkness as Willy softly reminisces about the Ebbets field game. "[Biff was] like a young god. Hercules—something like that. And the sun, the sun all around him. . . ." Miller often uses the slow, smoking cigarette to express a kind of thoughtfulness and solitary feeling in his characters. At the outset of act two, in *After the Fall*, Quentin also is moving in darkness and "a spark is seen, a flame fires up . . . he is discovered lighting his cigarette."

Things do not simply end and begin when the playwright sections off movement into acts and scenes. Often there are shifts of power between characters, realizations of broader, more frightening factors underpinning gesture and remark, confrontations which in one way or another turn dramatic event but do not lie easily discernible in the minute or two before intermission. Although coming near the end of the play, Ann's letter from Larry in *All My Sons* illustrates the gigantic effect of a single object on the meaning of anything previously enacted. The scene is powered like a nightmare game of "telephone." Each character, as he or she absorbs the message, is savagely torn out of innocence, real or imagined, and launched into a sadder, more complex but philosophically larger world.

Less the total cause of realization and more the supporting evidence in the difficult journey toward it, a rubber hose in *Death of a Salesman* becomes both a symbol of Willy's profound wish for release and, in Biff's hands, a potent psychological weapon. When he finally finds his truth and begins its painful articulation near the play's end, Biff flings down the hose to force Willy's deepest attention, shouting, "all right, phoney! Then let's lay it on the line." By mixing gesture, object and language, Miller signals us on a rational and on an instinctual level into an interaction not previously attempted in the play. . . .

Characters Defined by Surrounding Objects

Miller's imagination holds other, more obvious tricks. Both the repetition of the flute music and the reappearing angular presence of the apartments give notice throughout *Death of a Salesman* of serious intensity at work. The former device enters at moments when Willy feels especially drawn to a vision of past hopes and we sense freedom in his dream, a frontier get-rich-quick grace we can imagine in the music itself. The latter lights up menacingly when Willy feels haunted, overburdened, hopeless. "They boxed us in here. Bricks and windows, windows and bricks. . . ." A similar thing, of course, happens in *After the Fall*, the horrible tower looming its guilty, historical weight above Quentin's head throughout the play. Willy Loman, too, is caught in his own inescapable cycle of guilt. But predictably, his is little, personal. He can't get rid of the ghost of silk stockings, symbol of his infidelity, and thus, cause of Biff's distrust. It is simply amazing to me that whole years of experience and emotion can be caught in a single object and flung into the text so potently. It strikes me as powerful partly because it is the way memory works. Such gestures give a psychological clarity and texture to motivation that we recognize instantly. It is almost as if Miller has told us a story so well, he needs only to mention one aspect of its delivery for us to gather its full force again, and be moved.

But he knows greater symbolic tricks. With well-chosen objects Miller tips us off to the inner substance of his characters, or at least what they appear to be to the main figures whose viewpoints often shadow the plays. Holga, for instance, in *After the Fall*, is continually directed to hold flowers, at one point wanting to fill the whole car with them and, one foresees, Quentin's questioning, colorless life. During Willy Loman's hopeful moments in *Death of a Salesman*, Linda is cheerful and young, forever entering and exiting with ribbons in her hair, perpetually the "good sport" smiling over the laundry. People should, perhaps, be judged by their highest thoughts, their kindest behavior, but in Miller's world, and ours, they *are* what they hold, or wear, or buy or want. In *A View from the Bridge*, Eddie at first allegedly objects only to Rodolpho's fondness for what he considers transient and flashy items—motorcycles, records, the bright glitter of Broadway. Of course, he has deeper motives for his distaste, but Eddie feels comfortable listing his reasons in concrete, seemingly rational terms, just as we feel comfortable and omniscient seeing through them. Objects, in Miller's hands, are often a lens into the rather murky business of making characters rounder and fuller and, finally, living. We get to the point quickly that way; relation is set up and we can get on with the changes that larger drama promises.

But what is that larger promise? Here, probably, is the basic question one circles endlessly when discussing the impressive bundle of work some playwrights have produced. Miller undoubtedly handles his objects with discrimination and power on a theatrical level—how scenes themselves "play," when and how characters find and test their options in the social muddle of duty and affection—all these patterns wind themselves up and down around the natural orientation of things. Bits of the real world we find so convincing on the stage seem to be "real toads in imaginary gardens." Or just real pegs to hang a coat on. One can say Miller is a "great" playwright because when using these tools or toads or pegs, he takes them beyond mere mechanics into thematic richness. . . .

Characters as Objects

Often Miller uses his "thing characters" temporarily, for small effect in characterizing more important figures, much as a painter adds a side blur of color to create a setting for what he really sees. Happy, the cavalier Loman in *Death of a Salesman*, speaks of ladies as if their pursuit were a game, like bowling. "I just keep knocking them down. . . ." Quentin, in *After the Fall*, might agree. "Why do I keep sniffing the past?" he asks. "Except—there did seem some duty in the sky. I had a dinner table and a wife—a child. . . ." That particular wife, Louise, claims what he wanted was a comforter, a worshipper. "I'm not a praise machine," she objects. Yet there is little in the text itself to make her develop beyond the one-layered grouch she appears to be in Quentin's presence. She remains, for us, a thing, a machine—perhaps not a praise machine, as she says, but a flat figure who exists only to show us another avenue into Quentin. The thematic point in using such short-hand for Louise and others is that through that sketching, the main characters are developed into the kinds of figures who actually see people in terms of their usefulness in a specific world. Happy and Quentin make their egocentricities more and more apparent as one "thing" leads to another. In Happy's case, it is a natural leap from a man who treats women as nighttime toys to the man who could walk out on his hysterical father in a public place, claiming it's not his father at all, but just "a guy." . . .

The situation of Catherine in *A View from the Bridge* illustrates an odd plotting idea in the wider, thematic use of things. To ruin Rodolpho in her eyes, Eddie insists she is simply a passport ticket for him, American bait, just a useful item to be discarded as soon as citizenship opens. It seems an effective argument at first because Rodolpho is presented as an enthusiastic collector of glamorous objects carrying little value beyond the moment they fill. It becomes clear, however, that Eddie's understanding is a bit reversed. It is he who views Catherine possessively, as a thing to be, at least psychologically, had and controlled. It is Eddie who becomes the angry god watching his handiwork drop down the drain. He tells Alfieri, "I worked like a dog twenty years so a punk could have her?"

Miller handles a similar idea in his later play, *The Creation of the World*. But here, the angry god is a real god and the handiwork kicked downstairs to the waiting Satan is man—in toto—mankind. Perhaps this is the largest working of things thematically: [people] are not only manipulated by forces grander, more knowing than themselves, they are invented by them. This seems just more obvious and not too far from, say, a Willy Loman who invents a specific Ben in his imagination so he will have a hiding place when hope dies in the real, outer world. But in *Creation*, people have refused to act like things, or at least they have refused god's peculiar version of

how human things should behave. For this, they are condemned out of perfection, out of Paradise and thrust into a
difficult, weary life.

Broken Things Represent Broken Dreams

The life of a Willy Loman? Paradise evaporates and is that
what awaits us on the barren plain? In its eerie and powerful
movement, perhaps *Death of a Salesman* makes Miller's most
ambitious attempt at defining twentieth-century man caught
in western, industrial confusion. As we are guided through
Willy's splintering reality, we catch sight of the vast, oppressive
clutter which weighs so heavily on his world, reducing it—at
least in Miller's eyes—to meaninglessness.

Item one: everything is breaking down. If it's not the refrigerator, it's the car or the washing machine or the vacuum
cleaner. "I'm always in a race with the junkyard," Willy complains. But more than just objects seem to be flying apart. The
salesman's dream of a world where experienced old men keep
their power, sitting in robe and velvet slippers in hotel suites,
dialing in thousands of sales in a single morning, is a fantasy
that comes crashing around Willy almost audibly as he quar-
rels with Howard for a less exhausting job. It is a highly symbolic scene, almost unbearable to read or watch because
Howard, faced with his human machine and his inhuman
one, clearly prefers the latter. Before the suffering Willy, he is
oblivious, cheerfully possessed with his new toy, the tape recorder clicking on and off, bringing the voices of his family
grotesquely into the room.

Such monstrous thoughtlessness turns people into even
less than things. Willy argues against the assumption, pointing
to years of hard work, and loyalty and fatherly affection as
evidence of his personal worth. "A man is not a piece of fruit,"
he exclaims. "You can't eat the orange and throw the peel
away." But Howard is unconcerned with his appetite or his
manners, as are, by implication, the millions like him in posi-

tions of power in industrial America. To such intelligence, people are, first to last, tools, useful toward production, toward profit. Beyond that, they are not even pathetic, they are invisible.

The scene in the office ends with a terrible meaning. Howard leaves the room, and Willy slips into a fantasy plea to Howard's dead father, who once owned the firm. As he leans over the desk, arms imploring, he accidentally clicks on the tape recorder and jumps back, terrified of its life: the ridiculous rendition of states and their capitals in a child's nasal voice. "Howard!" Willy screams in near breakdown, "Howard!" as if left alone and helpless in the room with a killer. . . .

Such a killer mysteriously haunts the sealed-windowed set of *A Memory of Two Mondays* as well. We hear of a dark, dense area above the warehouse room, full of bins, the bins stuffed with used auto parts: mufflers and Marmon valves, ignitions, differentials, Locomobile headnuts. We can imagine blackened treasures no one remembers or cares to remember, parts of a whole almost impossible to understand. The weight of this room presses on the action, the physical presence of industrial complexity multiplied to madness. Under it, Gus's desperate litany of his long years with the place seems especially poignant. Who will remember him? Times themselves are no longer known because of their people, but because of the machines those people produce. Gus's realization forces him back to a final dream: to die flashy and well.

The Fatal Inflated American Dream

That final dream remains crucial to Miller and the visual, concrete form it takes in his hands makes, especially in *Death of a Salesman*, for stunning and memorable theater. After rejection by both Howard and his son, Willy purchases seeds—carrots, peas, beets, lettuce—and proceeds by flashlight in the middle of the night to plant them. "Nothing's planted. I don't have a thing in the ground," he worries, buying them, the remark multiplying to reflect upon his whole life of work and love. But as he gets happily to the job, he begins his mad discourse with the make-believe Ben, planning for a logical, lucrative suicide. It seems fitting that such painful thinking should take place in the garden: real earth, solid earth inviting essential meditation as the human world sags apart. We feel instinctively that Miller's choice of the whole business—the seeds, the hoe, even the darkness—is terrifyingly correct and implies a despair no longer even social, but now, desperately solitary. It represents Willy's and perhaps our own deepest wish back to the simplicity and the cyclical wholeness gardens symbolize, and the move comes with great power now in sudden contrast to the abstract complexities and cruelties of urban spirit. In this dense inner world, Willy yearns to grasp the real, the concrete and, through that, the release as Ben more and more lures him with diamonds, diamonds. "I can see it," Willy says, "shining in the dark, hard and rough, that I can pick up and touch with my hand. Not like—like an appointment!"

Yet, in Miller's world, even dreams become absurd, their baggage at last, heavy and silly and seemingly impossible to get rid of. Willy's dream land of big games and diamond mines and assistant buyer positions might be more beautiful than his actual everyday life, but as Biff slowly realizes, its self-inflation is eventually fatal.

Death of a Salesman in China

Arthur Miller

Arthur Miller is one of the most important dramatists of the twentieth century. He is best known as the author of Death of a Salesman *and* The Crucible.

In 1983, Miller was invited to direct a special staging of Death of a Salesman *in Beijing, China. The play had been translated into Mandarin Chinese, but Miller wanted the staging and look of the play to be decidedly American. Miller grappled with numerous political, cultural, and material differences between the West and China during the play. Among the greatest difficulties was explaining the tragic elements of the play to the actors, to whom it was unclear why Willy Loman wanted to commit suicide and how he expected his suicide to help his family. Miller found himself explaining everything from American business culture to how a gas heater works to the concept of private life insurance.*

The time has come to open the cardboard box I brought from the States with the football, helmet, and shoulder guards. Actors love distractions, and we now collect another little crowd of them as I help [the actor playing] Biff into the helmet and place the shoulder guards on him. He has an open, charming smile, looks Mongolian to me, very dark skin and a tall, straight horseman's body. He is about mid-thirties, with a rather pear-shaped lower face expanding out around the jaw hinges. Still, he is handsome. There is some fooling around in the helmet and shoulder guards, which ends with us all seated again and talking about salesmen.

Arthur Miller, *Salesman in Beijing*, New York: Viking Press, 1984. pp. 14–16, 51–56, 84–88.

"Actually," Ying [codirector Ying Roucheng] begins, "I think they will know what a salesman is." Why has he changed his mind?

Biff, sitting in an armchair in the helmet and shoulder guards, says, "The city is full of salesmen now, they're all up and down the streets."

"But that's different from the traveling salesman, isn't it?" I ask.

There is a silence. They seem themselves to be trying to understand their own city in a new light. The actor who will play Charley speaks, a tall, thin man, one of the best-known actors in China, who is on television a lot and recently starred on stage in the title role of *Ah Q*, based on the beloved Lu Xun's story; he is about fifty but looks younger and has the gentlest of voices. I cannot really place him as the gruff, ignorant, and peasantlike Charley, Willy's best friend, but he does have the personal warmth the part needs and perhaps we can build on that. He and Ying are the "senior members" of the company, along with Zhu Lin, our Linda, who is in her late fifties. "I think," he says, "that the people are learning about the West very quickly now. I don't think we have any *traveling* salesmen, but there are many privately owned small shops now—"

"And they give much better service," Ying adds, wryly. The laughter at this is significantly charged—no step can apparently be taken without political implications. What I find so interesting is that they, along with me, are trying to figure out where the country is at this moment [1983]. Ying originally, in New York, had said there were no salesmen in China, suggesting that the audience would have a hard time understanding the play, but that was more true then than it is now, less than a year later, and so he has had to change his mind. It seems more and more likely, to me, that public receptiveness to this play is as much an unknown to them as it is to me.

Actors Grapple with Concept of Insurance

Zhu Lin—Linda—interrupts: "We have no insurance in this country." Ying has now moved in to interpret in Shen's [dialect] instead; with him beside me I forget altogether that I am not understanding the Chinese instantaneously; he is but a breath behind the speaker, with not a single hesitation. Zhu Lin, I have been given to understand, is one of China's biggest stars, a surprise since she has no airs, nothing theatrical about her at all. She is wearing the standard outfit, blue buttoned-up cotton jacket and trousers. Her black hair lightly streaked with gray is bobbed to her nape. A deeply serious if not mournful face that can instantly change to a laughing one. She turns to Ying for his confirmation. "I am not sure about the insurance being understood. Especially about him dying for it." And then she turns to me. "Will they pay even though he kills himself?"

"Very likely. It is hard to prove it is not a car accident, after all."

And so we have our second cultural problem. But my faith seems not to have been disturbed, although I do not know why not. I think if they play from the heart it will go over. But I am still suffering jet lag, I remind myself. . . .

Explaining Insurance to the Audience

Ying Ruocheng's biggest worry now is that the audience will not understand how life insurance works and, hence, Willy's suicide in order to bequeath money to Biff. There is nothing like life insurance in this country, at least there hasn't been. But I have just read in today's *China Daily* that a company was organized in 1980, the People's Insurance Company of China, that has been doing a fabulous business insuring property and vehicles as well as crops in transit. On a trial basis they are now offering a pigeon-raising policy and have even begun testing life insurance in several provinces. The Western notion of a gratifyingly all-covering social security system turns out to be far from the facts. Older citizens are often in great need even by Chinese standards. Ying is surprised and happy to learn about insurance but still intends to explain how it works in the program notes. These, as in German theatres, are carefully read here and often are elaborate essays on the play. But salesmanship and insurance are at the heart of Willy's situation; how can an audience enter into the play without knowing about them? . . .

A New Cast Member

Ying the magician has produced another Happy [to replace the actor originally cast for this role], whom he has sprung from a play in rehearsal. This man, I now learn, was his original choice but had been tied up in a film when our rehearsals began. Best of all, he is obviously an old laughing-buddy of our Biff, who now horses around with him, guffaws frequently, and in general behaves like Biff with his brother Happy. . . .

Understanding Willy's Death

With our new Happy I go through the whole play from the beginning to block him into his positions, but I hardly need open my mouth; the other actors move him with a gesture as required, or he himself senses where he should be positioned. This is one part of the Chinese actors' training that I much appreciate: every one of them assumes he is responsible, provided the director agrees, for positioning himself logically on the stage. I have never seen this done with such ease and certainty, although I do change their moves about half the time. But mine are mostly small adjustments for the sake of a finer clarity of meaning or for emphasis in a script that is still, after all, about another civilization. In a play of their own I doubt they would have to be told very much at all about the blocking. By the end of the first three-hour session Happy has become part of the whole, although of course with the script still in his hand. He will study all day tomorrow, Sunday, and

I expect he will come in with the whole part learned on Monday. I cannot help marveling, when in addition it is all in Chinese! This is not a mere quip—for it must be a painfully uncertain process for these actors to slip into not only alien characters but an exotic way of life of which they know next to nothing. For example, Willy is desperate, yet he owns a refrigerator, a car, his own house, and is willing to "settle" for sixty dollars a *week!* And those were the fat dollars of decades ago. This, in China, is nothing short of fantasy. It is, incidentally, for this sort of reason that Ying, responding to a question at our press conference, said that the play cuts two ways as propaganda, for if a man can have reached Willy's standard of living and still feel in bad straits, it can't be as awful a system as is sometimes advertised.

But of course such numbers have little weight in putting together a picture of any reality here. Foreigners are still charmed by Chinese cities in which most of the inhabitants bathe from a single cold-water tap in the courtyard and have to use a public latrine the smells from which could float the Graf Zeppelin. If one is charmed by the housewife carefully emptying a tin bowl of dirty water into the street, it is well to remember she is doing this because there is no drain at all in her house. And those who walk the lanes of Beijing after the dinner hour may find it heartwarming to see young parents patiently tending small romping children in front of their houses, but their serious purpose is to get the tykes to defecate or pee on the open ground before bed. But they are indeed patient and loving even if there is little question they would prefer their own toilets.

Explaining a Gas Heater

What is turning out to be universal—unless I am going to be brutally disappointed on opening night—is emotion rather than "facts." Linda, for example, is thoroughly on target now, no longer Willy's whimpering doormat. She has told me that she had the wrong idea of the woman to start with. Instead, she has become, as he calls her, "my foundation and support," who is fighting off his death from the outset, the only one who knows that he has attempted suicide and has connected a device to the gas heater that, should the mood overtake him completely, he might use. Linda's part has often been weakly played, as though she were a mere follower, but that is un-likely to happen when the actress keeps herself aware of what the script has told her she knows. The "fact" in this case is a completely exotic gas heater for water, something that these Chinese have never seen (and, indeed, has probably ceased to exist anymore in the States) but which they easily understand once I describe its design and operation. In any case, its strangeness does not for an instant interfere with our Chinese Linda's eventual understanding of the kind of woman she has to play—the kind who is strong by concealing her strength. Perhaps we conventionally overestimate the profundity of technology's impact on our lives.

The Play's Tragedy and the Actors' Experiences

It rained all day, and in the evening we took Linda in our car instead of letting her find one of the last buses home. As we rode, she in the back seat with Inge, who interpreted for me, she told of the time in the 1940s when the Japanese were rav-aging Beijing and she had to hide her little daughter under a blanket to keep her from being taken and murdered by sol-diers. "The blanket was suddenly handed to me by an Ameri-can. He stayed by me till the troops had gone away. He re-fused to accept it back. I will never forget him." That was forty years ago. What burnings, rapes, horrors has she witnessed— this lady who often plays queenly parts in the grand Chinese manner with glittering robes and golden crowns and fingers covered with rings, and now Linda Loman in her little Brook-lyn house—how many women are in her? No wonder she hardly reacted when I kissed her on the cheek after her so affecting rehearsal performance of the Requiem—what was this achievement compared with some *real* scrapes she'd gotten through alive? But—I have now grown accustomed to this—Chinese simply do not react to praise in any open way, although they adore it like anyone else. Inge, in fact, thinks Americans are the only ones who respond to a compliment with a thank-you, all other peoples affecting to downgrade their achievement rather than to openly acknowledge it—in bad taste.

I have taught Biff, who had never laid eyes on an American football before, to throw a tolerable spiral pass to Happy—something I want them to do in the scene of Willy's homecoming in Act One. Unfortunately his aim is not always that great, and this afternoon, while I was busy looking at a lighting diagram, he threw one across the stage and hit Linda square in the jaw. She refused not only aid but any of our attempts to comfort her, although the shot must have hurt. Biff, who has a manly, stoical nature, did not so much rush over as walk in a purposefully rapid stride to her and apologize. I thought to ease the moment by saying that she was the one who ought to be wearing the helmet I had brought from America and that she was now the first football injury in Chinese history. She is a great lady who was able to laugh, and there was never a flash of resentment against Biff at the accident. The ball, on my unfortunate instruction, is pumped up hard.

A Student Responds Emotionally to *Death of a Salesman*

Meredith Kopald

At the time this article was published, Meredith Kopald was an English teacher at Eldorado High School in Albuquerque, New Mexico.

In the following selection, Kopald writes of her experiences teaching literature, particularly her practice of asking students to respond freely and emotionally to what they have read. The results were often passionate and sometimes therapeutic personal responses. Kopald taught Death of a Salesman *in this way, and found that the play elicited strong reactions from students. One student in particular was deeply affected by the relationship between Willy and Biff, seeing his father in the character of Willy and himself in Biff. Eventually approaching his father with what he had learned from his interpretation of the play, the student reconciled with him, claiming Miller should be awarded a Nobel Peace Prize.*

Teachers are not therapists. Nor do we wish to be. Nevertheless some learning *is* therapeutic, particularly expression of strong feelings which are evoked when students recognize themselves or their situations in literature. Students create these connections for themselves: in the struggle to engage a piece of literature, they often encounter art intimately in terms of their own lives and their own struggles with identity.

I know what students are feeling because I ask them to write reaction papers. "Take out a piece of paper," is my most frequent instruction. "Write a reaction to your first meeting

Meredith Kopald, "Arthur Miller Wins a Peace Prize: Teaching, Literature, and Therapy," *The English Journal*, vol. 81, March 1992, pp. 57–60. Copyright © 1992 by the National Council of Teachers of English. Reprinted with permission.

with Vladimir and Estragon in *Waiting for Godot.*" "Respond to the first paragraph of *Pride and Prejudice.*" "When Marlow asks the listeners on the *Nellie*, 'Do you see him? [Kurtz] Do you see the story? Do you see anything?'" I ask students to write what *they* see, what they understand at this point in Joseph Conrad's *Heart of Darkness*. My copies of the novels and plays I teach are marked with: *Stop Here. Write.* And often I scribble the question I will suggest they address in their responses.

These informal, hastily-written reactions do not substitute for polished papers written outside of class or for in-class essays. Rather they are opportunities for students to sort through a myriad of impressions before discussion. These papers often give students a chance to identify what disturbs them, or what does not make sense, good places for discussion to begin. When, for example, my Advanced Placement class studied *Hamlet*, Michael wrote,

> I am Hamlet. He, like me, is a procrastinator on a grand scale, and this causes him enormous guilt. The guilt feeds the lack of self-worth and that feeds the procrastination—an endless circle.

Class discussion of the reasons for Hamlet's delay was led by Michael whose identification spurred his curiosity.

Identifying with Literature

Despite our appreciation and delight when students respond personally to literature, as teachers we are not often sure what to do when reactions describe real problems. "When I was ten years old my father committed suicide." How do we respond to this confidence? As a teacher? As a therapist? Do we say, "Your sadness over Willy's suicide recognizes the climactic power of his death, which was prepared for throughout the play?" Or do we say, "I'm so sorry to hear about your father?"

Shannon, an Advanced Placement student, wrote,

> I know who my Kurtz is! She's been a nemesis for three
> years, and it finally struck me what kind of hold she has on
> me, and it is most frightening. She has the voice of Kurtz—
> beautiful, melodic, and she is wonderfully talented for hold-
> ing the spotlight but there's nothing underneath, just a con-
> fused pettiness and cruelty. She holds court, you know, and
> keeps me close, just like Kurtz and Marlow. For a while, I
> was afraid I was turning into her.

Should we respond, "Your comment perfectly captures the
seductive connection between Marlow and Kurtz in *Heart of
Darkness?*" Or should we try to save a friendship?

Over the years I have found ways of responding that work
for me. For the majority of papers, the best thing to do is to
do nothing at all. These reactions work their magic without
teacher response. I read their papers quickly during lunch or
between classes, then have a classroom aide file them in individual folders to be returned at the end of the year. If the responses are personal, I feel successful. Literature should move
us, should make us aware of the human condition. Sometimes, however, a more serious therapeutic response is needed.
Three or four students have written about incest, potential
suicide, or painful struggles with sexual identity. In these cases
I make immediate referral to the school counselors. I tell the
students privately and in person something like, "I read what
you wrote yesterday, and it scared me. I don't want you to
hurt yourself or to feel such intense pain. Because I am concerned about you, I asked the counselor to call you into the
office, so you can talk about these issues. You don't have to
feel this pain alone." No student has ever refused counseling
or resented my interference. I believe these disclosures were a
call for help.

Miller talks to actor Dustin Hoffman during production of the 1985 CBS Television adaptation of Death Of A Salesman, *in which Hoffman portrayed Willy.* Hulton Archive/Getty Images.

Death of a Salesman Ignites Therapy

Several years ago, my practice with reaction-papers well-established, I asked students to write during our study of Arthur Miller's *Death of a Salesman*. Senior Jason Dalton's first response was written after we had listened to the Lee J. Cobb recording and before our planned second reading in class.

> I feel sad. My father is Willy. He's searched all his life to make money. He wants to be a millionaire. He went to summer school until the 8th grade to learn how to read. He became a damned P.E. teacher then he quit for business. In 9 years 7 jobs. Seven damn jobs. And he wants me to be a success.
>
> P.S. When we read I'd like to be Biff.
>
> Jason "Biff" Dalton

Jason was clearly taken by the play. He did indeed read Biff and his best friend read Willy; the two boys turned their desks to face each other. Each day, at the beginning of fourth period, Jason strode into the room, waving aside classroom formalities: "Don't take roll, Mrs. K., everyone's here," he announced and took up his position. "Shhh," one girl whispered to another, "Jason's working something through." His second reaction paper was written the day we finished our in-class reading.

> I hate Willy. I feel really bad about how he ruined everyone's life. He is despicable and disgusting. Why did he do it? Willy has no redeeming qualities. Why? How can there be such people on the earth? I don't know any of this, but I am happy about Biff and I hope I can be like him. I have a salesman for a father and he is not a father, he is a salesman. Much of the hatred I feel for Willy I feel for my father. He treats me just like a Biff—the only way I can get his attention is to tell him what a success I am and I am a success through little or no help from him. My mother's name is Linda but luckily she did not buy his dream and divorced him. Willy deserved to die so he would set Linda free. If I were Biff I'd burn the twenty thousand dollars. It is too much of Willy's. Hap is the most pitiable character. Willy absolutely ruins his life because he feeds him full of his despicable American Dream crap and Happy sits there and buys it because that is the only way he can be a success in his father's eyes.
>
> P.S. Thank you for letting me read Biff.

Analysis of the Play and of the Self

The Friday before winter break, fourth period entered my room prepared to write an in-class literary essay. I passed out the questions and watched them settle down. All except Jason. He squirmed and fidgeted and finally came up to my desk. "I'd like to write another reaction instead of an essay," he announced. I hesitated just a moment before assenting. So, while his classmates wrote critical essays, Jason completed his drama.

He gave it a title.

Death of a Salesman: A Falling Safe upon the Head of an Unsuspecting Victim

Arthur Miller's play *Death of a Salesman* struck me on a very tender nerve. A nerve that until now I was aware of but not really in touch with. I was not able to deal with my pain and anger until we read this play. The tender spot I'm speaking of is my virtually nonexistent relationship with my father. I see many parallels between myself and my father and the Loman family. My father is a salesman. He, too, is much happier with a batch of cement. I feel a very strong "can't get near him" feeling with my father. The only way I can get and hold his attention is to tell him of all my accomplishments. We are not close as Willy and Biff are not. I dislike Willy a great deal and this dislike stems from my anger and disappointment in not being close to my father. At the end of this play I was made acutely aware of this anger and disappointment.

All my life I've tried and tried to be close to my father, failing every time. We are just two totally different people. The play moved me so much and made me so aware of the way I felt that I made a decision last night not to go and visit my father in his new home in Minnesota for Christmas. I called his house and he was on a trip. I left a message and he called me later. We talked and talked. For almost half an hour my anger poured from my body into his. When I finished and we had both broken down in tears, I told him everything I had ever wanted to tell him. After my anger had all spewed out, for the first time in my entire life I felt love toward him. *For the first time!!* I feel I have grown up in a very big way. I think I have done in 17 years what took Biff thirty-four.

All of this because of a play, a bunch of words printed on paper. How can a play do this? Genius, I say!! *Death of a Salesman* is the greatest piece of literature I've ever read.

Never before have I felt this way about a book. I feel so greatly in debt to Arthur Miller. His insight into the feelings of middle class America has greatly inspired me. My Christmas present to my father will be a copy of this book. I know it will hit home to him also. I'm very glad we read this and who said that high school students cannot identify with this play? It hit me over the head with a very big stick. And Arthur Miller deserves a Nobel Peace Prize for starting peace between myself and my father.

Salesman Provokes Reconciliation

As I read Jason's paper, I felt first fear, then guilt, then overwhelming relief that everything had turned out all right. It took me a while to appreciate his achievement: both emotional and rhetorical control over his grief and anger and a full sense of reconciliation with his father. From a psychological point of view Jason recognized and expressed his powerful feelings: sadness, anger, disappointment, loss, reconciliation, and reunion. The opportunity to rehearse an alternative to rejection, rebellion, and alienation from his father came when Jason read Biff's part in the play. Biff's struggle is to confront his father, and this Jason found easier to do than did Biff, perhaps because he learned from Biff's courage. To confront their fathers, both sons find that they must confront themselves by telling the truth. Biff says, "you're going to hear the truth— what you are and what I am! . . . I am not a leader of men, Willy, and neither are you." Jason faces up to the fact that he has a "virtually non-existent relationship" with his father. When he writes, "We are just two totally different people," he simultaneously separates from his father and accepts their differences. I have no way of knowing, of course, what it meant to Jason to read Biff's lines,

> Why am I trying to become what I don't want to be? What am I doing in an office, making a contemptuous, begging fool of myself, when all I want is out there, waiting for the minute I say I know who I am!

But surely, what informs Jason's writing is his love for his father, his desire to be close to him, and his recognition that he is a separate and different human being. These understandings are what maturing is all about. I believe Jason when he says, "I feel like I have grown up in a very big way."

Emotions from Literature Affect Writing Style

This episode reinforced my conviction that strong feelings and potent writing go hand in hand. Note, for example, the crisp comparison, "I think I have done in 17 years what took Biff thirty-four." Notice also the forceful spondaic rhythm and repetition of "For the first time!" The details, too, are arresting. My heart goes out to Jason's father who listened to his son and then broke down in tears. And the reader is moved by Jason's concluding tribute to Miller who "deserves a Nobel Peace Prize for starting peace between myself and my father." It is not just the power of Jason's feelings but his ability to express them in eloquent and vivid language that makes this a memorable piece of writing.

A Real Biff Finds Peace Through Literature

Miller once wrote about his "disappointment" that "the self-realization of the older son, Biff, is not a weightier counter balance to Willy's disaster in the audience's mind." He needn't have worried. When I sent him Jason's papers, he responded immediately: "Thanks so much for sharing [Jason Dalton's] reports. They moved me deeply. It is for this kind of enlightenment that one hopes, to deepen the self-understanding of people."

After he graduated I saw Jason three more times. The first winter he returned from the United States Naval Academy and told me with some pleasure that when he visited his father, "He made me put on my uniform and walk around to impress the neighbors." That June, he talked about the girl he was dating and his summer job in Los Alamos. The following spring he sat restlessly beside my desk and said, "I shouldn't have come home. I should be lying on the beach in Fort Lauderdale." We both knew it was time he moved on.

I have long believed that we teachers do not choose the students who use us in the therapeutic way; they choose us, and they let us go when they no longer need us. They choose us from some urgent need of theirs and because the literature we teach taps some deep longing within them. They choose us because something we say or do makes us safe for private disclosures. When they reveal their secrets to us, they seek neither sympathy nor pity and certainly not advice. They are redefining themselves through literature and testing new definitions in the powerful privacy of personal writing. Reacting to literature in this way does indeed, as Miller said, "deepen self-understanding" and in the sense of healing and growth is a therapeutic experience.

Contemporary
Perspectives on Suicide

Suicide Rates Rise Across the Globe

The Economist

Founded in 1843, The Economist *is a weekly publication covering current events, politics, economics, science, business, and the arts.*

In the following viewpoint, the authors explain that while suicide is a global phenomenon, its root causes may lie in highly individual combinations of cultural, social, and personal factors. Among students in India, for example, causes of suicide may include the high-pressured academic atmosphere, while in Japan social pressures to be part of a group may be a factor. The authors discuss the growing influence of the Internet on suicide and also assert the need for government intervention programs to lower suicide rates.

For many people in the northern hemisphere, the spirits lift in June—but in India it is a time for examination results, and they can bring despair as well as joy. In any event, the Sneha suicide-prevention centre in Chennai stays open round the clock in mid-June, and the telephones have been ringing hard. Suicide rates have been rising in India, especially among the young, and over a third of those who kill themselves are under 30 years old.

But suicide is a mysterious phenomenon; it defies generalisations. Emile Durkheim, the father of modern sociology, wrote in 1897 that suicide rates were a key sign of the state of a community. It was commonest, he reckoned, at two extremes—highly controlled societies, or loose, atomised ones. Since then, his successors have filled thousands of books with theories about what makes people take their own lives: the negative factors which remove the desire to live, and the positive ones that can make self-killing an attractive or even "fashionable" option.

In India, the desperation of students has been studied relatively little compared with that of farmers, who have killed themselves in rising numbers in recent years: over 17,000 died by their own hand in 2003. The trend is often ascribed to debt, drought and the ready availability of pesticides that serve as poison.

But in India no less than elsewhere, the inner turmoil that makes people end it all usually has complex causes: social dislocation, family tensions or long-term depression. No group escapes. The country's suicide capital is booming Bengalooru (Bangalore), where most of those who do it are skilled workers; housewives are the next-biggest category. Some reports say suicide became common among Indian farmers only in the late 1990s, after agrarian and trade reforms introduced a few years earlier by a liberalising government. In truth, such deaths were probably going unrecorded for decades before that. Official data tell us as much about social mores (the extent to which self-killing is concealed) as about what really happens.

Suicide Pacts and Plans on the Internet

But one new trend that is clearly pushing the real incidence of suicide up is the growing use of the internet to learn about, plan or even encourage self-killing. Back in 1997, the internet was used to publicise the effectiveness of charcoal-burning barbecues as a means of carbon-monoxide poisoning; the first recorded case of two or more people using the web to form a suicide pact was in Japan in 2000. Since then hundreds of people, if not more, have taken their lives this way, in countries from Australia to Spain.

Nowhere are such internet deaths more common than where they started—in Japan, whose suicide rate has long been among the highest of never-communist developed countries. Japan is a conformist society, and life, it is said, is bleak for those who do not fit in. It has a tradition of self-killing, which in some forms, such as the ritualised *seppuku* ("belly-cutting") of the samurai, may still be deemed honourable, even noble. Public figures shamed by scandal often kill themselves. For anonymous losers, the internet may provide a means to become, in death at least, a part of a group, so important in Japanese society. Typically, two or more such people bent on suicide will make contact via a website, get together on an appointed day and end their lives with exhaust or charcoal-stove fumes while parked in a deserted spot, perhaps facing Mount Fuji.

South Korea, too, has seen a new wave of such suicides. It, like Japan, is a country in which the young find themselves under huge pressure to succeed, and most internet pacts involve young people. Unlike Japan, however, South Korea does not have a long tradition of self-inflicted death. Two decades ago it had a fairly low suicide rate (under ten per 100,000 in the 1980s), but now it has one of the world's highest (24.7 in 2005). And whereas in Japan internet pacts form only a tiny proportion of the total number of suicides, some studies suggest they may account for almost a third in South Korea. In both countries, though, most people who kill themselves are elderly or middle-aged men.

Social and Economic Factors Affect Suicide Rates

For all their elusiveness, suicide rates can certainly be correlated with other social and economic indicators. The Organisation for Economic Co-operation and Development, a Paris-based think-tank for rich countries, says the same range of factors explains cross-country differences in people's declared degree of contentment with life, and suicide rates. So four-fifths of the variance in suicide rates across 50 countries can be explained by differences in the rates of divorce and unemployment, in quality of government, religious beliefs, trust in other people and membership of non-religious groups.

All this may help to explain why so many ex-communist countries have high suicide rates (over 13 per 100,000) and so many Latin American countries have low ones (under 6.5), but some differences are nonetheless striking. Among rich countries, the high rates of Hungary, Japan, Belgium and Finland stand out, whereas most Mediterranean countries score low (below five). Ireland has a significantly higher rate than its neighbour, Britain.

Certain differences can be readily explained. China is one of the few countries in which more women kill themselves than men. Over half the world's female suicides are Chinese; among Chinese under 45, the female rate is twice the rate among males. Why should things be different in China? Part of the explanation clearly lies in the high rate among rural women, which in turn may be partially explained by the ready availability of poisons (weedkillers and pesticides), and the absence of any effective treatment. Similar apparent anomalies may be explained by the ready availability of other poisons. Many Sri Lankans kill themselves by eating the seeds of the yellow oleander, a common shrub.

Intentional self-poisoning with these seeds was almost unheard of in Sri Lanka before 1980, but in that year two girls committed suicide by eating them. Inadvertently, they started a trend. Similar fashions often follow the suicide of a celebrity such as Michael Hutchence, an Australian pop star who apparently took his own life in 1997, or M.J. Nee, a Taiwanese actor who hanged himself in 2005.

Governments and Social Agencies Can Help

Measures can be taken to make it harder for people to kill themselves. They may not be able to (and arguably, should not try to) stop the really determined, but they can save the lives of many who are confused, temporarily depressed or in need of sympathetic attention. In countries like Britain, suicide rates have fallen significantly thanks to legislation that allows drugs such as paracetamol to be sold only in small quantities. South Korea has tried to close "death websites", suicide chatrooms, internet bulletin boards and blogs, and Japan also tries to police the web. Andrew Cheng, a Taiwanese professor of psychiatry, wants to alert the media to the risks of glamorising celebrity suicides. In South Korea barriers have been erected in metro stations, to stop people throwing themselves in front of trains.

Government action certainly makes a difference, though sometimes results are perverse. Some Indian states pay bereaved families compensation for the loss of a breadwinner who has killed himself; this seems to increase the suicide rate.

At a more practical level, higher barriers could be put up on San Francisco's Golden Gate bridge, off which some 1,250 people have leapt to their deaths since it opened in 1937; tests in May showed that such barriers are quite feasible. And many places badly need suicide-prevention agencies like the Samaritans, which offer a friendly response to anyone contemplating taking his own life. Mental health gets a low priority in many countries, including places like Japan, with high suicide rates.

In most rich countries, though, rates have been falling for the past two decades, especially among the elderly. In poorer places the picture is more mixed. In most of Africa no reliable data are available; elsewhere, especially in places where traditional roles are undergoing rapid change, suicide seems to be increasing. Worldwide, indeed, suicide rates have increased by 60% in the past 45 years. About 1m [1 million] people a year die at their own hands. Too many of these deaths are avoidable.

A Documentary About Suicide Sparks Debate

Killian Fox

Killian Fox is a British journalist.

In the following viewpoint, Fox examines filmmaker Eric Steel's 2006 documentary The Bridge, *which chronicles one year of suicides—and attempted suicides—at San Francisco's Golden Gate Bridge. The film includes interviews with family members of victims and with those who have pondered or attempted suicide at the bridge. The film, which depicts actual suicides, has been called graphic and a "snuff movie," but it has also been described as sensitive, realistic, and gripping. Fox asserts that depression and suicide issues are often kept out of public discourse and acknowledges that some commentators believe* The Bridge *may be able to bring needed attention to this seldom-discussed topic.*

The Golden Gate Bridge in San Francisco is the most photographed man-made structure in America. It is also the world's leading suicide location. More than 1,250 people have thrown themselves off the bridge [as of February 2007] since it opened to the public 70 years ago.

In the opening minutes of a controversial new documentary, we watch as a man stands on the Golden Gate walkway, staring down at the water 67 metres [218 feet] below. Coming to a decision, he hoists himself over the low railing and gains a foothold on the other side. A moment goes by and then, before our eyes, he pushes away into mid-air. We watch him fall. Four entire seconds stretch out before the splash.

Killian Fox, "Death in America," *New Statesman*, vol. 136, February 19, 2007, pp. 40–41. Copyright © 2007 New Statesman, Ltd. Reproduced by permission.

Suicides on Film

It's a shocking start to a film that has caused outrage since word of it began to filter out [in 2006]. A first-time director named Eric Steel trained a number of cameras on the Golden Gate throughout 2004, capturing all but one of that year's 24 suicidal leaps from the bridge on camera. The press got wind of the story and, before Steel's film had even been screened, it was being denounced as "irresponsible", "exploitative", "voyeuristic", "ghastly" and "immoral". One commentator labelled it a "snuff movie".

Men and women do fall to their deaths on screen in *The Bridge*—six in total—but Steel argues that those who come to see it for voyeuristic reasons will leave disappointed. The film is more concerned with the circumstances that led to each jump, which it explores through interviews with witnesses and people close to the victims. "Each splash," says Steel, "sets in motion a very intimate journey into a person's life."

Jumpers Drawn to Golden Gate

These splashes occur with sickening regularity. Tad Friend, the staff writer at the *New Yorker* whose 2003 article "Jumpers" inspired Steel to make the film, described them to me as "a very steady metronome of people jumping off the bridge—about one every two weeks". This ratio does not take into account the failed attempts, thwarted by police patrols and passers-by, nor the many deaths that go unreported every year.

"Jumpers are drawn to the Golden Gate because they believe it's a gateway to another world," says Dr. Lanny Berman, executive director of the American Association of Suicidology. "They think that life will slow down in those final seconds and then they'll hit the water cleanly, like a high diver."

"The bridge has a false romantic promise to it," says a friend of Daniel "Ruby" Rubinstein, one of the jumpers in the film. Ruby couldn't afford health insurance, and ended up begging his friends for antidepressants. "Maybe, walking out there, he had a romantic moment or two . . . But hitting the water can't have been fun."

"It is a violent, vile, terrible, murderous death," 24-year-old Kevin Hines tells me. "People believe that you just hit the water and disappear into the abyss and then you die. But in reality, it's painful and it lasts a long time." He should know. Severely bipolar, Hines went through a particularly black episode in September 2000, when he was 18. He had seen a website that pinpointed the Golden Gate as an effective place to commit suicide, so the next morning he took a bus there. He paced back and forth along the walkway for 40 minutes, weeping openly. A German woman asked him to take her photograph. He obliged, then thought to himself, "F--- it, nobody cares," and vaulted over the railing.

"The second my hands left the bar, I realised I didn't want to die," he says. Somehow, he manoeuvred himself into an upright position and endured the 120kph [75 mph] impact. Splinters of bone from his lower lumbar region flew up into his organs but missed his heart, and he became one of 26 people who have survived the plunge. "Do you want to know why the Golden Gate is such an attraction for people trying to end their lives?" Hines asks. "It's the four-foot rail."

Ever since the bridge was completed in 1937, people have been campaigning for a suicide-prevention barrier. Friend highlighted the issue in his *New Yorker* article, noting that, over the years, proposed barrier solutions have been rejected by the Golden Gate board for aesthetic and financial reasons. He believes that *The Bridge* has pushed the campaign forward. "It has had an immediate practical effect, and in that way alone I think it's a very important film." Steel is less certain. "if you stop the jumps," he says, "people will probably find other places to end their lives. It requires a more global approach. You have to fix the problem at the bridge, but you

A sign marks the spot of a crisis counseling phone on the Golden Gate Bridge. Steel's documentary opened a debate about why there isn't a suicide barrier on the famous landmark. Justin Sullivan/Getty Images.

also need to come up with better ways to deal with mental illness and suicide prevention in the community. One without the other is pointless."

In 2004, as Steel and his crew were filming the Golden Gate, 32,439 people killed themselves in America. By contrast, there were 17,357 homicides that year. The rate of suicides continues to stand at almost twice the murder rate. If this statistic is widely known in the United States, it is not reflected in the media. News outlets tend not to report suicides for fear of provoking copycat attempts—a justifiable fear in San Francisco, where countdowns to the 500th and 1,000th Golden Gate fatalities in 1973 and 1995 sparked jumping frenzies. Nor does suicide receive much coverage in the arts, and the furor generated by Steel's film, one of few recent attempts to raise questions about suicide on screen, supports the notion that the subject is taboo.

Ethical Debate over Documentary

"In documentaries about gang violence, or Rwanda, or anything not involving suicide, showing death on screen is OK," says Hines. "But if it's about doing it to yourself—that's untouchable." Part of the problem, in his view, is the stigma attached to mental illness. "Even people in mental health can be prejudiced," he says. "I have to live with it every day. Because I'm labelled as bipolar and I did what I did, I must be a complete psychopath." Hines has nothing but praise for Steel's film. He is adamant that, rather than glorifying death at the bridge, the film is an effective deterrent, and he hopes it will go some way towards breaking the silence.

The Bridge may be a force for positive change, but certain troubling ethical issues remain. When Steel applied for a shooting permit in November 2003, he concealed his true intentions, pitching a study of the "spectacular intersection of monument and nature that takes place every day at the Golden Gate Bridge". The friends and families of those who jumped, whom Steel interviewed while the shoot was still under way, were also kept in the dark.

"I couldn't risk word getting out and having someone die as a result of the film," Steel says. "Clearly, there are people who are unbalanced and who would be seeking attention in the worst possible way. I had to have enough faith in my own sensibility and my ability to be respectful with the footage."

Even if the authorities had agreed to the actual project, media pressure would have halted the shoot within days. It is clear, however, that the director's decision to dupe people connected with the suicides is the weakest link in an argument for an already controversial project.

When news of the film broke, some of the interviewees spoke angrily to the press. Now, unexpectedly, they are becoming Steel's strongest line of defence. Following a screening for friends and families in San Francisco [in April 2006], one of them—Mary Manikow—retracted her complaint that she had been "used", saying she felt "positively pleased" to have been involved with the film. Another, Matt Rossi, gave the film-maker a tearful hug and thanked him for making it.

Suicides Increase After Film Debut

The Bridge premiered at the San Francisco Film Festival at the end of April [2006]. In May, four deaths and 11 attempted jumps were reported by the Golden Gate board, which wasn't slow to blame the increase on extensive coverage for the film. The director is unrepentant. "From my experience, April to June was always the worst period at the bridge," he says. "Of course the authorities want to make me the bad guy here. But the only way to stop suicides is to put up a barrier. The answer is not to stop showing the movie."

Friend agrees. "Since the bridge's status as a suicide magnet is hardly a secret, people are going to continue jumping off it even in the absence of media attention. Perhaps, rather than ignoring the problem, one should try to address it." Steel is quick to emphasise that the camera operators, who were planted on either side of the bridge at a considerable distance from the walkway, alerted bridge patrols whenever they believed someone was planning to jump. He claims that six deaths were averted as a result. "I guarantee there has not been a film made about Iraq in which the film-maker can say they saved six lives."

The Marin County coroner, Ken Holmes, announced [in January 2007] that at least 34 people died at the bridge in 2006. A study of suicide deterrents (the eighth undertaken by the bridge board to date) has yet to reach a decision. And meanwhile, at a steady pace of about one every two weeks, the jumps continue to happen.

The Ethics of Physician-Assisted Suicide

Renske Heddema

Journalist Renske Heddema is a frequent contributor in various media in the Netherlands and Switzerland.

In the following selection, Heddema reports on Switzerland's emerging—and comparatively loose—euthanasia laws. Many who suffer from various diseases—some terminal, others not— travel to Switzerland to end their lives with the assistance of a physician. Heddema focuses not only on the ethical issues posed by "suicide tourism," but also on Switzerland's history of assisted suicide and attempts in other European countries to grapple with the issue.

In 2002, I was in the process of setting up an interview with Ludwig Minelli, a lawyer and founder of the suicide-assistive organisation Dignitas. Returning my call, he asked whether I would be free this very morning. Handing over the phone to somebody else, he told me a 'compatriot' wished to speak with me. A Dutch woman came on the line.

Anna (whose real name has been withheld) spoke with difficulty, as if she were drunk. She said Minelli had just accompanied her, along with her husband, to the Dignitas doctor in Zurich. Intimidated, I asked if she was in Switzerland to end her life. She said she was.

She then invited me to meet with her at the Dignitas apartment. Two hours later, I sat at her bedside in the one-room apartment, my microphone on.

The woman was 44 years old, but looked older. Her face and hands were bloated and she was in obvious pain. For

Renske Heddema, "One-Way Ticket to Switzerland," *Swiss News*, vol. 5, May 2007, pp. 16–19. Copyright © 2007 *Swiss News*. Reproduced by permission of the author.

years, she had suffered myriad diseases that took all the joy from her life and placed a burden on her family, she said.

In spite of the pain, she chose words with precision and seemed both intelligent and strong willed. She seemed to know exactly what she wanted.

Although none of her diseases had been diagnosed as 'terminal', she'd had enough. She'd explained the decision to her two young daughters in Holland and expressed relief that she would die in a few hours.

Defining Deadly

The Swiss have long made a practice of turning to associations of volunteers when they wished to end their life.

At least two charitable organisations offer this form of suicide assistance: Exit has helped Swiss residents since 1982. The association has a list of some 50,000 members who pay a yearly fee to ensure future services.

But it was not until Dignitas began reaching out to clients abroad in 1998 that other nations began to focus on the liberal euthanasia practice in Switzerland. Dignitas has some 7,000 members; a majority of them are foreigners.

Both insist on a rational and premeditated decision by the patient. Much is done to document the illness in advance, but the on-call physician at the clinic has final discretion.

The attending doctor may insist on medical reports that recovery is not possible, and is at liberty to refuse a patient even though organisational guidelines do not make terminal illness a precondition of assistance.

Premeditated and Rational

Anna did not waver. No doctor had wanted to help her at home, so she was grateful for the Dignitas option. Her husband, speaking softly with her, clearly respected her decision.

173

But the Dignitas doctor-on-call was not persuaded to proceed. That morning, he had required medical confirmation from her doctor in Holland of the brain tumour and its impact.

Perhaps he was uncomfortable with the fact that she was only 44. Regardless, as time wore on, it became evident that the Dutch specialists weren't sending the confirmation she would need.

Minelli and one of his co-workers waited by the fax. Phone calls went back and forth. Eventually, Minelli and I said goodbye to the couple.

When I called the next day, Minelli told me the papers had not arrived and the couple had returned to Holland. He was matter-of-fact about the situation. For her part, Anna did not rule out a return trip.

Dignitas and Exit

The pre-conditions imposed by Dignitas and Exit have become increasingly similar in recent years. Like Dignitas, Exit has begun considering some patients with Alzheimer and psychiatric disorders along with the elderly whose pain and disability have taken their will to live.

Both associations insist that the patient be rational. Their wish to die must be premeditated and declared in writing.

A camera is set up to record the patient taking the drug themselves—firm evidence that it was not administered by clinic staff. Witnesses are present and local authorities are always informed.

Peaceful and Painless

So, the biggest difference between Exit and newcomer Dignitas seems to lie in the fact that the latter helps foreigners who travel to Zurich to die.

A foreigner can face weeks or months of medical scrutiny before they fly in. On arrival in Zurich, the Dignitas doctor consults with the patient and decides whether their determination falls within legal boundaries.

*Former physician Jack Kevorkian made headlines as a champion of terminally ill patients'
right to assisted suicide. Between 1990 and 1998, he assisted in the deaths of nearly one
hundred people, and was convicted of second-degree homicide in 1999.* AP Images.

They can always back out, but if the doctor agrees to proceed, they are taken to the apartment and given an anti-nausea drug. Thirty minutes later they are handed a bitter, colourless drink of sodium pentobarbital at three times the lethal concentration.

In five minutes they will lapse into a coma and the heart will stop, in what is apparently a peaceful and painless death. The coroner and police are called. Dignitas charges about SFr [Swiss francs] 1,800 for assisting a suicide.

'A Way Out'

But Exit alleges that Dignitas doesn't take enough time in its process, and foreigners essentially die on demand. The organisation says assisted suicide should not be directed from a distance.

Even though a patient's case is thoroughly vetted by Dignitas over a period of weeks or months, he or she will stay in Zurich for a maximum of 24 hours.

The idea of a patient flying in, going directly to the Dignitas doctor and then to the Dignitas apartment to die, remains for many people incompatible with the sober reflection that should be associated with the end of life.

Dignitas founder Minelli says the very possibility of 'a way out' helps many people cope with their illness and ultimately reject the option.

Tradition of 'Self-Aid'

Assisted suicide in Switzerland has a peculiar history. During the First World War the Swiss military stood at the Swiss borders for four long years. On returning home, they often found their businesses or farms had gone bankrupt. In their agony and shame, some chose to kill themselves or to ask a comrade to shoot them.

In 1918, Swiss Parliament conceived a law to help regulate this practice: a person who for selfish reasons helped somebody end his life would face up to five years in jail. By contrast, those who helped a friend to die for altruistic reasons did not break the law. Respect for the practice was enshrined in Article 115 of the Swiss criminal code in 1941, allowing Swiss citizens to develop an efficient system of so-called 'self-aid'.

The creators of Exit used this legal basis to set up the first Swiss association for assisted suicide in 1982. Exit asked doctors to write the prescription for a deadly potion, but kept the entire procedure outside the medical and judicial field.

As a result, the practice co-existed within Swiss democratic traditions, where citizens are sovereign and have the final word in politics and in matters affecting their lives.

Dignitas Opens an Office in Germany

After a schism developed within Exit, former member Ludwig Minelli started his own agency in 1998. Minelli is a 74-year-old lawyer with a bent for public relations. As secretary general of Dignitas, he has recently sparked debate concerning mercy killing in Germany, opening an affiliate in Hanover in 2005 and appearing on German talk shows.

German law prohibits euthanasia, which is a suicide where a person dies at the hand of another, but does not make it a crime to help someone kill himself.

But the country's medical association opposes all forms— passive and active—and has explicitly condemned Dignitas' activities. Germany's doctors are not allowed to assist in suicide and people visiting the Hanover office of Dignitas must still travel to the Zurich office in order to die.

Dignitas Has Faced Criticism

In Great Britain—where assisted suicide is a criminal offence carrying a 14-year sentence—Minelli's activities have been equally well documented. After providing access to the Dignitas apartment in the initial years, resulting in various BBC [British Broadcasting Company] documentaries, he received a delegation from the British parliament in 2005 and addressed the Liberal Party Convention in Brighton in September 2006.

To date, Dignitas has assisted in the deaths of some 700 individuals, around ten per cent of them British citizens. But it has faced sharp criticism. One opponent is Exit, which believes Dignitas could trigger a legal clampdown that could threaten its own existence.

Referring to Dignitas as 'a dying agency', Exit's communications officer Andreas Blum says that it is only a matter of time before the Swiss Justice Department intervenes to stop the service to foreigners. Blum feels that the unwanted publicity generated by the Dignitas practice will bring an end to the liberal legislation in which Exit has been able to operate and develop.

In that way, he says, "the organisation and its leader massively damage the cause for which we stand."

The general prosecutor of Canton Zurich, Andreas Brunner, complains that the canton's image could be tarnished by an international reputation for suicide tourism. He was disappointed [in 2006] when the Federal Council judged the existing legislation sufficient and Justice Minister Christoph Blocher ruled out any amendment as "capitulation".

Minelli Responds to Criticism

Minelli responded to criticisms of Dignitas in a broadcast interview in February [2007]. He stressed that after 700 assisted suicides, he had "an absolutely pure conscience".

In a vast majority of cases, said Minelli, patients choose to continue their life.

Specialist staffers work as volunteers to ensure there can be no conflict of interest. Membership contributions are low (there is an introductory fee of SFr 100, followed by a SFr 50 minimum per year), and Dignitas operates as a non-profit organisation. Initial accusations that Minelli is breaking the law by making a profit have faded.

Nonetheless, attempts to discredit Dignitas won't stop any time soon. "Opponents are trying to make it difficult for doctors to work with us," Minelli says.

European Shift

In the meantime, Minelli's ongoing battle against legal restrictions at a European level seems to be bearing fruit. In February 2007, the Swiss Federal Court ruled that the European Convention on Human Rights provided the basis for an autonomous decision by the individual concerning death, implying that Dignitas can rightly assist patients with psychological diseases or a considered wish to leave this world for other reasons.

The European legal framework would equally make obsolete any condition that an illness be terminal. The current state of affairs is likely to pave the way for a European expansion of Dignitas, rather than signalling a halt to its Swiss operations.

It could also mean a return trip to Zurich for Anna. A few months after she was refused by Dignitas, I contacted her to find out how she felt about the experience.

She said returning to a life of disability had been difficult, and her children and former caregivers had also had difficulties. Her condition had not improved and she continued to struggle.

Nevertheless she spoke highly of Minelli: "I lived my life with dignity" and want to go out the same way, she said. Dignitas takes that wish seriously and in that way, it addresses an important need in and outside Switzerland, she said.

Involvement Therapy Helps Suicide Survivors Cope

Bob Condor

Bob Condor is the editor of Seattle Conscious Choice, *for which he writes about the environment, personal health, and social issues. He also regularly contributes to the* Seattle Post-Intelligencer.

In the following viewpoint, Condor discusses how a family eases the shock and sadness from a son's suicide by retelling his story. Though the issue of suicide is often considered taboo in society, the family is determined to tell their son's story while speaking of the importance of involvement therapy, prevention programs, and the warning signs of a suicidal mentality.

For two years after his 16-year-old son Trevor committed suicide, Scott Simpson's stomach churned and flipped and ached. He called his stomach "totaled."

For six months, Simpson woke up wondering, "Will I make it through today?"

"The next question I asked myself was, 'Do I want to make it through today?'" said Simpson, a framing contractor in Edmonds [Washington]. "Some days I wasn't so sure."

Like a lot of parents who face such a tragedy, Scott and Leah Simpson asked themselves a lot of questions in the aftermath. They didn't see Trevor's suicide coming. Their son was a star athlete and honors student with a 3.95 grade-point average. He died in early 1992.

"It was a total shock for our whole family," said Leah Simpson. "We have two other children, one older and one younger. We all asked, 'Why did this happen to us?' and 'Why didn't we know?'"

Bob Condor, "Living Well: Retelling Story of Son's Suicide Brings Healing," *Seattle Post-Intelligencer*, April 17, 2006. Reproduced by permission of the author.

Suicide as a Taboo Subject

Scott Simpson went to Trevor's school to look for answers. He didn't find many. In fact, his practical nature kicked in and he approached school officials about starting a suicide prevention and awareness program. He was politely advised to, well, maybe, let's just start a scholarship fund instead.

It seemed there were too many "stigmas and taboos" attached to teen suicide, said Scott, even though suicide is the second-leading cause of teen death in [Washington]. Only accidents kill more adolescents.

The Simpsons call it "deadly silence" and bring up the topic of suicide when they get the chance. They will be featured speakers at the 18th annual "Healing After Suicide" national conference in Seattle April 29, [2006].

Breaking the Silence

The all-day event, scheduled at the Grand Hyatt Hotel, is co-sponsored by the Suicide Prevention Action Network USA and the American Association of Suicidology (the study and researching of suicide). It is an opportunity for survivors, support group leaders and caregivers to come together.

The Simpsons will be speaking about "involvement therapy" for suicide "survivors." It will require retelling Trevor's story yet again, which doesn't faze either parent.

"I have a really good friend who asks me regularly if I want to relive Trevor's suicide, why our family wants to revisit the topic," said Leah. "The main thing, I answer, is every time I go out and talk about Trevor, it is an opportunity to affect someone. They might see themselves or a loved one in what I am saying."

A List of Signs

There is a list of signs that indicate when people are in acute risk for suicide, including talk or threats about wanting to kill or hurt themselves, or talking or writing about death out of context. Researchers call this "ideation" and suggest it is reason enough to contact a mental health professional or the national hot line for a referral.

Other warning signals are increased use of alcohol or drugs, expression of no purpose or reason for living, anxiety, inability to sleep or sleeping all the time, a feeling of being trapped, withdrawing from friends and family and uncontrolled anger and rage.

Involvement Therapy

Scott Simpson said involvement therapy helps survivors to open up about their loss and deep feelings of guilt.

"Lots of survivors say to themselves [the suicide] has to be over and done with, that they aren't going to talk about it anymore," he said. "The problem is, there are millions of neurons in the brain that are still linked to the name of the loved one. When Trevor's name was mentioned after it first happened, all I felt was sadness and grief. Now, when I hear 'Trevor' I might think about the Trevor Simpson Suicide Prevention Award (which goes to a school program each year)."

Involvement therapy is a technique for coping with life after a loved one commits suicide. Simpson said there are three steps:

1. Involve yourself in good memories of the suicidal person, providing more positive inventory for those brain neurons.

2. Volunteer your efforts to work toward suicide prevention.

3. Attend meetings of a suicide support group for survivors.

"We have conducted a pilot study to show involvement therapy helps people recover from suicide," said Simpson. "Survivors have to be the ones to speak out. We all need to be more educated about suicide."

Suicide Prevention Programs

To their credit, the Simpsons pressed and lobbied the state Legislature during the mid-1990s to establish formal suicide-prevention programs in state schools. [Washington's] Youth Suicide Prevention Program represents a prime example of their son's legacy and his parents' willingness to break the more typical silence associated with teen suicide. The program is considered a model for other states.

The conference will feature a number of workshops, and presentations will add to the suicide education effort. Researchers known as suicidologists have compiled a growing body of research and statistics. Some examples:

- About 30,000 Americans commit suicide each year, and there are 25 attempted suicides for each death.

- Feelings of hopelessness (that there is no solution to a personal problem) are found to be more predictive of suicide risk than a diagnosis of depression.

- Based on data from 1979 to 2003, we can estimate that the number of survivors in the United States is approximately 4.5 million.

Simpson recalled a past conference during which one researcher explained that suicide can be compared to a slot machine.

"He said, 'The sevens all have to line up perfectly,' including the biological factors, the sociological factors, the emotional factors and extensional factors," said Simpson.

A major obstacle for any suicide survivor is getting past the guilt stage.

"You never get away from the guilt completely or [from] thinking what if," said Simpson during an interview. "Just this morning I was thinking if I had taken Trevor with me to work that day like I had first planned, it would have changed everything."

Raising Awareness of Elder Suicide

Ezra Ochshorn

Ezra Ochshorn is a social worker at the Florida Mental Health Institute in Tampa.

In the following selection, Ochshorn notes that prolonged illness, physical limitations, dependence on a caretaker, and the death of life partners are some of the profound life changes many older people face. Ochshorn asserts that these significant events are too often viewed as normal parts of aging, leaving many seniors with undiagnosed, untreated depression and an increased risk of suicide.

If you ever want to bring a discussion of serious health issues to a screeching halt, simply utter two words: elder suicide. I repeatedly experienced this when talking with fellow students and mental health professionals during my years in graduate school and while working as a counselor on hospital psychiatric units.

Although suicide-prevention programs have proliferated in recent years, almost all attention has been directed at teenagers. This national focus ignores a basic fact: Seniors have the highest suicide rate of all age groups. While people aged 65 and older comprise only 13 percent of the US population, they account for 19 percent of all suicides. The suicide rate in 1999 among 15- to 24-year-olds was 10.3 per 100,000, while among the aged it was 15.9 per 100,000 (almost 50 percent above the national average). This statistic translates into a total 6,000 elder suicides, and most experts believe the actual, unofficial number is considerably higher.

Ezra Ochshorn, "Elder Suicide: Are You Aware of It?" *The Christian Science Monitor*, June 2, 2003. Reproduced by permission of the author.

Why has this issue received so little publicity? I believe the answer lies in our youth-obsessed society's fear of aging. This contributes to ageism—a belief that the elderly are inferior and people to be kept out of sight and mind.

As a result, the struggles of older people are given short shrift in American life.

Depression Is Not a Natural Part of Aging

There is also widespread belief that depression—considered the greatest risk factor for suicide—is a natural part of aging for which there is no remedy.

Certainly there are life circumstances that can hit the elderly especially hard, such as physical illness, loss of family and friends, and the need for care. But depression is not linked to aging itself, and most seriously depressed seniors respond well when their problem is acknowledged and treated.

Yet proper treatment occurs all too rarely. Most general physicians have little if any training in evaluating suicidal risk among the elderly.

This is significant because research indicates more than 70 percent of seniors who kill themselves see a physician within the preceding month, and most give verbal or behavioral clues as to their deadly intentions.

Physicians are not alone in this regard. For example, the vast majority of social workers, who provide half of all mental-health services in this country, have no specific geriatric training. It is predicted there will be an acute shortage of specialty trained doctors, social workers, and other health professionals over the coming decades as the elderly grow to represent an unprecedented proportion of the US population.

Although many Americans view suicide as a taboo subject—particularly when not concerning teenagers—it will not magically disappear if ignored.

Recommendations for Combating Elder Suicide

The number of older Americans is expected to double by 2030—and unless the issue receives serious attention, suicides can reasonably be expected to increase accordingly. Here are some suggestions for change:

- Increase public-health efforts to raise awareness of elder suicide. This should include discussion of social, economic, health, and psychological risk factors that lead to suicide.

- Increase the number of health and mental-health professionals trained to work with seniors. This may require providing incentives such as scholarships and loan-forgiveness programs for those who choose a geriatric concentration.

- Combat the stigma many seniors associate with receiving mental-health treatment.

- Develop and fund community treatment programs for the elderly. Everyone should be entitled to accessible and affordable mental-health services.

- Most important, the ageism that permeates American culture must end. It is only when everyone is regarded and treated as unique and valuable that suicides will decrease. Regardless of age, people with purposeful lives, good self-esteem, and a supportive environment rarely choose to kill themselves.

For Further Discussion

1. Robert A. Martin's essay in chapter 2 argues in favor of salesman Willy Loman's status as a tragic figure. Considering Aristotle's concept of tragedy as only affecting nobility, and using examples from the play, support your opinion of whether Willy's suicide is a tragic act.

2. In chapter 2, Meredith Kopald writes of a student's therapeutic response to *Death of a Salesman*. Using examples from the play and one article on suicide from chapter 3, compare and contrast Willy's situation to the issue of suicide today.

3. The interview between Arthur Miller and Paul Solman in chapter 1 and the excerpt from Miller's *Salesman in Beijing* in chapter 2 shed light on the universal impact of *Death of a Salesman*. Using information from these two selections and examples from the play, make an argument as to why Miller's play is successfully staged throughout the world and across generations.

4. Sighle Kennedy's essay in chapter 2 asks, "Who Killed the Salesman?" Referring to this essay and specific examples in *Death of a Salesman*, discuss your opinion of what provoked Willy Loman's suicide.

For Further Reading

Edward Albee · *The American Dream*. New York: Coward McCann, 1961.

Edward Albee · *Who's Afraid of Virginia Woolf?* New York: Atheneum, 1962.

Edward Albee · *"The Zoo Story" and Other Plays*. London: J. Cape, 1962.

David Mamet · *Glengarry Glen Ross*. New York: Grove, 1984.

Arthur Miller · *After the Fall*. New York: Viking, 1964.

Arthur Miller · *All My Sons*. New York: Reynal, 1947.

Arthur Miller · *The Crucible*. New York: Viking, 1953.

Arthur Miller · *A View from the Bridge*. New York: Dramatists Play Service, 1956.

Eugene O'Neill · *The Iceman Cometh*. New York: Random House, 1946.

Eugene O'Neill · *Long Day's Journey into Night*. New Haven, CT: Yale University Press, 1956.

J.D. Salinger · *The Catcher in the Rye*. Boston: Little, Brown, 1951.

Charles Webb · *The Graduate*. New York: New American Library, 1966.

Tennessee Williams · *A Streetcar Named Desire*. New York: New Directions, 1947.

Tennessee Williams   *Cat on a Hot Tin Roof.* New York: New Directions, 1955.

Bibliography

Books

Susan Rose Blauner	*How I Stayed Alive When My Brain Was Trying to Kill Me: One Person's Guide to Suicide Prevention.* New York: Harper Paperbacks, 2003.
Harold Bloom, ed.	*Death of a Salesman.* 2nd ed. Bloom's Modern Critical Interpretations. New York: Chelsea House, 2006.
Steven R. Centola, ed.	*Echoes Down the Corridor: Arthur Miller, Collected Essays, 1944–2000.* New York: Viking Penguin, 2000.
Diego De Leo	*International Suicide Rates and Prevention Strategies.* Cambridge, MA: Hogrefe & Huber, 2004.
Emile Durkheim, Richard Sennett, and Alexander Riley	*On Suicide.* New York: Penguin Classics, 2007.
Martin Gottfried	*Arthur Miller: A Life.* London: Faber and Faber, 2005.
Kay Redfield Jamison	*Night Falls Fast: Understanding Suicide.* New York: Vintage, 2000.
Helene Koon, ed.	*Twentieth Century Interpretations of* Death of a Salesman: *A Collection of Critical Essays.* New York: Simon & Schuster, 1984.

Paula T. Langteau   *Miller and Middle America: Essays on Arthur Miller and the American Experience.* Lanham, MD: University Press of America, 2007.

Eric Marcus   *Why Suicide?* New York: HarperOne, 1996.

Robert A. Martin and Steven R. Centola, eds.   *The Theatre Essays of Arthur Miller.* New York: Da Capo, 1996.

Arthur Miller   *Salesman in Beijing.* London: Methuen, 2005.

Brenda Murphy and Susan C.W. Abbotson   *Understanding* Death of a Salesman: *A Student Casebook to Issues, Sources, and Historical Documents.* Literature in Context series. Westport, CT: Greenwood, 1999.

Matthew C. Roudane   *Conversations with Arthur Miller.* Jackson: University Press of Mississippi, 1987.

Edwin S. Shneidman   *Comprehending Suicide: Landmarks in 20th Century Suicidology.* Washington, DC: American Psychological Association, 2001.

Periodicals

Marc Abrahams   "Suicide Isn't Penniless," *Guardian* (London), November 14, 2006.

Bart Barnes and Patricia Sullivan   "Playwright of Broken American Dreams," *Washington Post*, February 12, 2005.

Alex Berenson and Benedict Carey — "Experts Question Study on Youth Suicide Rates," *New York Times*, September 14, 2007.

E.J. Dionne Jr. — "Arthur Miller's Lessons," *Washington Post*, February 15, 2005.

David Klinghoffer — "Undying Salesman: Arthur Miller's 'Death of a Salesman,'" *National Review*, March 8, 1999.

Ilene Lelchuk and Erin Allday — "Parents Reflect, Schools Mobilize to Curb Suicide," *San Francisco Chronicle*, January 22, 2007.

George Monbiot — "We Are Making Our Children Ill with Unreasonable Expectations," *Guardian* (London), June 27, 2006.

Patricia Petralia — "To Prevent Teen Suicide, Understand It," *Washington Post*, February 15, 2007.

Susan Saulny — "A Legacy of the Storm: Depression and Suicide," *New York Times*, June 21, 2006.

Katharine Webster — "More than Hurt Feelings After Suicide: 'Devastated' Boston Founder," *Chicago Sun-Times*, March 26, 2007.

Index